THE ESSENTIAL GUIDE TO
ROOFING

WITHDRAWN

FROM THE EDITORS OF

JLC
The Journal of Light
Construction

hanley▲wood

THE ESSENTIAL GUIDE TO
ROOFING

Published by Hanley Wood
One Thomas Circle, NW, Suite 600
Washington, DC 20005

Distribution Center
29333 Lorie Lane
Wixom, Michigan 48393

THE JOURNAL OF LIGHT CONSTRUCTION
186 Allen Brook Lane
Williston, Vermont 05495

Edited by Clayton DeKorne
Illustrations by Tim Healey
Production by Theresa Emerson
For more information on The Journal of Light Construction or to subscribe to the magazine, visit www.jlconline.com

HANLEY WOOD CONSUMER GROUP
Group Publisher, **Andrew Schultz**
Associate Publisher, Editorial Development, **Jennifer Pearce**
Managing Editor, **Hannah McCann**
Senior Editor, **Nate Ewell**
Proofreader, **Joe Gladziszewski**
Vice President, Retail Sales, **Scott Hill**
National Sales Manager, **Bruce Holmes**

Most Hanley Wood titles are available at quantity discounts with bulk purchases for educational, business, or sales promotional use. For information, please contact Bruce Holmes at bholmes@hanleywood.com.

VC GRAPHICS
President, Creative Director, **Veronica Claro Vannoy**
Graphic Designer, **Jennifer Gerstein**
Graphic Designer, **Denise Reiffenstein**

10 9 8 7 6 5 4 3 2 1

Printed in the United States of America

Library of Congress Control Number: 2005932292

ISBN-10: 1-931131-51-1
ISBN-13: 978-1-931131-51-3

DISCLAIMER OF LIABILITY
Construction is inherently dangerous work and should be undertaken only by trained building professionals. This book is intended for expert building professionals who are competent to evaluate the information provided and who accept full responsibility for the application of this information. The techniques, practices, and tools described herein may or may not meet current safety requirements in your jurisdiction. The editors and publisher do not approve of the violation of any safety regulations and urge readers to follow all current codes and regulations as well as commonsense safety practices. An individual who uses the information contained in this book thereby accepts the risks inherent in such use and accepts the disclaimer of liability contained herein.

The editors and publisher hereby fully disclaim liability to any and all parties for any loss, and do not assume any liability whatsoever for any loss or alleged damages caused by the use or interpretation of the information found in this book, regardless of whether such information contains deficiencies, errors, or omission, and regardless of whether such deficiencies, errors, or omissions result from negligence, accident, or any other cause that may be attributed to the editors or publisher.

Acknowledgements

Several years ago, then Journal of Light Construction chief editor Steve Bliss assembled a group of editors to share thoughts on creating our own manual of best practice — the JLC Field Guide. We imagined this as a builder's trusty companion, ever present on the seat of the truck or in the toolbox, ready to answer the kinds of questions that come up on the job site every day.

Thanks to Steve Bliss, who envisioned, mapped, and directed the project in its early stages; to Clayton DeKorne, who expertly executed the work that Steve had started; to Tim Healey for illustration; to JLC staff editors Ted Cushman and Charlie Wardell, who compiled large portions of the original manuscript; to Josie Masterson-Glen for editorial production and copyediting; to Jacinta Monniere for the original book design; to Barb Nevins, Lyn Hoffelt, and Theresa Emerson for production work; to Ursula Jones for production support; and to Sal Alfano and Rick Strachan of Hanley Wood's Washington, D.C., office for executive management.

Finally, special thanks to all the authors and JLC editors over the years, too numerous to mention, whose work is the basis of this volume.

Don Jackson
JLC Editor

Introduction

Over the last 20 years, The Journal of Light Construction has amassed a wealth of first-hand, practical building knowledge from professionals who have dedicated themselves to custom residential projects. In the Home Building & Remodeling Basics Series, we have distilled this valuable knowledge into handy reference guides — selecting the critical data, fundamental principles, and rules of thumb that apply to strategic phases of residential building and remodeling.

Our intention is not to set building standards, but to provide the housebuilding trades with a compilation of practical details and proven methods that work for the many builders, remodelers, subcontractors, engineers, and architects who are committed to producing top-quality, custom homes. The recommendations we have compiled in these volumes usually exceed the building code. Code compliance is essential to building a safe home — one that won't collapse or create unsafe living conditions for the occupants. However, we are striving to reach beyond this minimum standard by offering a record of best practice for residential construction: details and methods used not only to produce a safe building, but to create a long-lasting, fine-quality home.

While it is not our first focus, we have made every effort to uphold the building codes. The prescriptive recommendations in this book are generally consistent with the 2000 International Residential Code and the Wood Frame Construction Manual for One- and Two-Family Dwellings, published by the American Forest and Paper Association. Although these standards reflect the major U.S. model codes (CABO, BOCA, ICBO, and SBCCI), regional conditions have forced some municipalities to adopt more stringent requirements. Before taking the information in this volume as gospel, consult your local code authority.

As comprehensive as we have tried to make this resource, it will be imperfect. Certainly we have strived to limit any error. However, many variables, not just codes, affect local building and remodeling practices. Climate variability, material availability, land-use regulations, and native building traditions all impact how houses are built in each city, town, county, and region. To account for every variation would require a database of understanding far greater than the scope of this book. Instead, we focus here on some principles of physics, design, and craftsmanship that won't change by region or style. It is our hope that these principles, used alongside the building code, will guide professionals toward a greater understanding of best practice.

Clayton DeKorne

Editor

How to Use this Book

This volume is intended to be used as a reference book for professionals and experienced homeowners with an understanding of basic construction techniques. It is organized in general order of construction, and within each section we have provided several navigational tools to help you quickly located the information you need, including a section headline at the top of the page, cross-references within the text, and references to Figures and illustrations.

Table of Contents: The two-page table of contents found on the following spread offers a detailed look at this book — featuring not just each section, but the individual topics found therein, along with page numbers for quick reference.

Index: A detailed index of the entire volume can be found at the back of this book.

Figures: When appropriate, tables, graphs, and illustrations have been added to help clarify the subject matter. Every effort has been made to place these Figures on the same page, or spread of pages, as the copy which references them. You will find references to Figures in bold in the text; in the event that the Figure falls on an earlier page or in another section, a page reference will be included in the text.

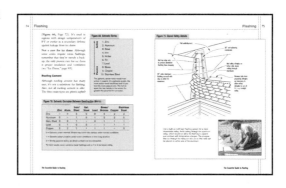

Be sure to pick up the other three books in the Home Building & Remodeling Basics Series for more valuable information that will help you get your next project done right:

- The Essential Guide to Framing
- The Essential Guide to Exteriors
- The Essential Guide to Foundations

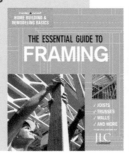
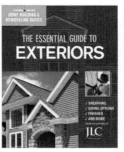
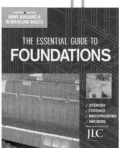

Table of Contents

Estimating Roofing Materials

Slope and Pitch

Slope is defined as a roof's vertical rise (in inches) per foot of horizontal run (**Figure 1**). For example, a 6:12, or "six-in-twelve," roof rises 6 in. for every ft. of run.

$$\text{SLOPE} = \text{RISE}/\text{RUN}$$

Pitch is different from slope; it's the ratio of rise to span. For example, a roof sloped at 6:12 has a pitch of ¼.

$$\text{PITCH} = \text{RISE}/\text{SPAN}$$

Flat Roofs

Even "flat" roofs should have some slope. To prevent pools of standing water, they should slope at least ¼ in. per ft.

Calculating Roof Area

Gable Roof Area

To find the length of a rake on a gable roof, multiply its horizontal distance (the roof's run) by the slope conversion factor in **Figure 2**, then multiply by the length of the ridge to find the area.

Figure 1. Slope vs. Pitch

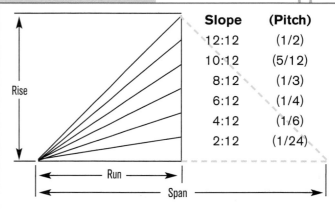

Slope	(Pitch)
12:12	(1/2)
10:12	(5/12)
8:12	(1/3)
6:12	(1/4)
4:12	(1/6)
2:12	(1/24)

Don't confuse "slope" and "pitch." Slope is in. of rise per ft. of run. Pitch is the ratio of rise to span.

Figure 2. Slope, Hip/Valley Conversion

Slope (in. per ft.)	Conversion Factor	
	Slope	Hip/Valley
4:12	1.054	1.452
5:12	1.083	1.474
6:12	1.118	1.500
7:12	1.157	1.524
8:12	1.202	1.564
9:12	1.250	1.600
10:12	1.302	1.642
11:12	1.356	1.684
12:12	1.414	1.732

Multiply a roof's run by the correct factor to get the length of its rake. To find the length of hips and valleys, multiply the correct factor by the horizontal distance of a hip or valley.

RAKE LENGTH = RUN x SLOPE FACTOR
GABLE ROOF AREA = RAKE LENGTH x
RIDGE LENGTH

Hip/Valley Length

To find the length of a hip or a valley, multiply its horizontal distance (run) by the hip/valley factor in **Figure 2**.

HIP OR VALLEY LENGTH = RUN x
HIP/VALLEY FACTOR

Material Quantity

Most roofing materials are sold by the square.

1 SQUARE = 100 SQ. FT. ROOF AREA

Order extra for hips, ridges, valleys, starter courses, and cutting waste, as described for each material.

Figure 3. Fasteners per Square

Roofing Type	Nail Type	Nail Quantity (per square)
Asphalt Shingles		
New roof	1 1/4" galvanized roofing	2 lbs.
Reroofing	1 1/2"–1 3/4" galvanized roofing	3 lbs.
Wood Shakes or Shingles*		
24"	4d shingle	2 lbs.
16"–18"	3d shingle	2 lbs.
Hand-split shakes	6d shingle	2 lbs.

* Note: Use only hot-dipped, stainless-steel, or aluminum nails for shakes and shingles. Do not use electrogalvanized or copper.

Estimating Underlayment

- **15-lb asphalt felt**: One roll (144 ft. x 36 in.) covers 4 squares using standard coverage (**Figure 7**, page 5) or 2 squares for half-lap applications (**Figure 8**, page 6).

- **30-lb asphalt felt**: One roll (72 ft. x 36 in.) covers 2 squares using standard-coverage, or 1 square in half-lap applications.

Estimating Asphalt Shingles

Most asphalt shingles are sold three bundles per square (assuming a 5-in. weather exposure). After calculating the appropriate number of squares for the roof field, add the following:

- Add 10% to the total roof area for waste;

- Add one square of shingles for every 100 lin. ft. of hips, valleys, ridges, and starter courses;

- Add up the lengths of all hips and valleys and divide the sum by 20. Then add this many sq. ft. of shingles for additional waste.

Estimating Wood Shakes and Shingles

A nominal square is four bundles, and a nominal square of shakes is five bundles, but this depends on the course exposure (**Figure 4** and **Figure 5**, facing page). The steeper the slope, the more shingle that can be exposed.

Figure 4. Wood Shingle Coverage

	Approximate Coverage of One Square (4 bundles) Weather Exposure (in.)								
Length & Thickness*	**3½**	**4**	**4½**	**5**	**5½**	**6**	**6½**	**7**	**7½**
16" x 5/2"*	70	80	90	100**	–	–	–	–	–
18" x 5/2¼"	–	72½	81½	90½	100**	–	–	–	–
24" x 4/2"	–	–	–	–	73½	80	86½	93	100**

* Sum of the shingles stacked; e.g., 5/2" means 5 butts = 2" thick.
** Maximum exposure recommended for roofs.

Adapted from Cedar Shake and Shingle Bureau

Figure 5. Wood Shake Coverage

		Approximate Coverage (sq. ft.) of One Square (shakes applied with ½-in. spacing)			
		Weather Exposure (in.)			
Shake type, length, and thickness	**No. of bundles**	**5½**	**7½**	**8½**	**10**
18" x ½" Hand split-and-resawn mediums	4	55*	75**	–	–
18" x ¾" Hand split-and-resawn heavies	5	55*	75**	–	–
24" x ½" Hand split-and-resawn mediums	4	–	75*	85	100**
24" x ¾" Hand split-and-resawn heavies	5	–	75*	85	100**
24" x ½" Tapersplit	4	–	75*	85	100**
18" x ⅜" Straight-split	5	65*	90**	–	–
24" x ⅜" Straight-split	5	–	75*	85	100**

* Maximum recommended exposure for 3-ply roof.
** Maximum recommended exposure for 2-ply roof.

Adapted from Cedar Shake and Shingle Bureau

- For starter courses, add one square for every 240 lin. ft. of eaves.

- For valleys, order one extra square per 100 lin. ft. of valley to account for waste.

Estimating Nails

To estimate nail quantities, see **Figure 3**.

Estimating Clay and Concrete Tile

- Field tile is usually sold in full pallets, and accessories in full boxes. Consult the manufacturer's information for the number of field tiles per square, the number of squares per pallet, and the number of tile accessories packaged per box.

- It takes about 90 concrete field tiles to cover a square of roof area when using a 3-in. top lap.

- Add 3% to field tile quantities for waste and breakage.

Asphalt Shingles

The term asphalt shingles refers to both organic-asphalt and fiberglass shingles. The main difference is in the mat, or base sheet. Unless otherwise specified, all references to asphalt shingles here include both types. For general information on asphalt shingles, refer to **Figure 6**.

Selecting Asphalt Shingles

When choosing asphalt shingles look for:

Organic vs. Fiberglass Mat

Asphalt shingles may have either an organic felt or fiberglass mat. Organic-mat shingles are generally thicker, more tear resistant, and better able to

Figure 6. Typical Asphalt Shingles

Configuration	Tabbed	Multi-Tabbed	Laminated	No Cutout
Width	12 to 13^{1}/4"	12 to 17"	11^{1}/2 to 14^{1}/4"	12 to 13^{1}/4"
Length	36 to 40"	36 to 40"	36 to 40"	36 to 40"
Low Slope(1)	2:12 to 4:12	2:12 to 4:12	2:12 to 4:12	2:12 to 4:12
Normal Slope	4:12 to 21:12	4:12 to 21:12	4:12 to 21:12	4:12 to 21:12
Steep Slope(2)	21:12 & beyond	21:12 & beyond	21:12 & beyond	21:12 & beyond
Exposure	5 to 5^{5}/8"	4 to 7^{1}/2"	4 to 6^{1}/8"	5 to 5^{5}/8"
Approx. ship. wt. per square	200 to 300 lbs.	240 to 300 lbs.	240 to 360 lbs.	200 to 300 lbs.
No. of shingles per square	65 to 80	65 to 80	64 to 90	65 to 81
Bundles per square	3 or 4	3 or 4	3 or 4	3 or 4
Fire/wind ratings	A or C fire rating; wind resistant	A or C fire rating; wind resistant	A or C fire rating; wind resistant	A or C fire rating; wind resistant
Life expectancy(3)	15-25 yrs.	15-25 yrs.	20-30 yrs.	15-25 yrs.

(1) See **Figure 8**, page 6.
(2) Use six fasteners per shingle and place two spots of quick-setting asphalt cement under each tab.
(3) Life expectancy depends on weight and tear strength of shingle.

Adapted from Cedar Shake and Shingle Bureau

Figure 7. Standard Underlayment (4:12 and steeper)

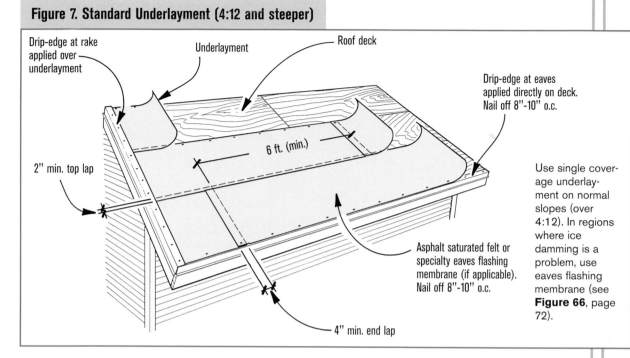

Drip-edge at rake applied over underlayment

Underlayment

Roof deck

Drip-edge at eaves applied directly on deck. Nail off 8"-10" o.c.

2" min. top lap

6 ft. (min.)

Use single coverage underlayment on normal slopes (over 4:12). In regions where ice damming is a problem, use eaves flashing membrane (see **Figure 66**, page 72).

Asphalt saturated felt or specialty eaves flashing membrane (if applicable). Nail off 8"-10" o.c.

4" min. end lap

withstand expansion and contraction. With a fiberglass shingle, a heavy mat or double-layer mat is desirable for added strength.

Shingle Weight

In an **organic-asphalt shingle**, weight is a good measure of shingle quality. A 210-lb. (per square) shingle should last about 15 years, a 230- to 240-lb. shingle should last 20 years and a 320-lb. shingle should last 25 years.

In a **fiberglass** or high-profile **"architectural"** shingle, however, weight is not a good measure of quality because the weight may be due to heavy mineral fillers that do not add strength.

Fire Ratings

Use only Class-A rated shingles for residential construction.

Tear Resistance

Shingle strength is largely a function of the quality of the mat and the quality of the asphalt. Use only ASTM D3462 rated shingles. Fiberglass shingles should also have a UL listing.

Reroofing

Over existing shingles, use traditional organic-asphalts, because they're thicker and much less likely than fiberglass to let the old roof "telegraph" through.

Underlayment for Asphalt Shingles

Codes and warranties require underlayment. It keeps the house dry until the roof is finished, provides an extra barrier against wind-driven rain and ice dams, and separates shingles from resins in wood sheathing.

Underlayment Weight

Roofing felt is classified by its weight per square. Use 15-lb. in the field and 30-lb. to line valleys. Thirty-pound felt is stiff and may telegraph wrinkles if used in the field.

Underlayment for Steep Roofs

On roofs 4:12 and steeper, use one layer of 15-lb. roofing felt, lapped at least 2 in. at overlaps and 4 in. at end laps (**Figure 7**).

Underlayment for Low-Slope Roofs

On roofs from 2:12 to 4:12, start with a 19-in. starter course, then lap succeeding courses by 19 in. (**Figure 8**). With a standard 36-in. roll, this will provide double coverage. For cold-weather treatment, see "Eaves Flashing," **Figure 66,** page 72.

Figure 8. Low-Slope Underlayment

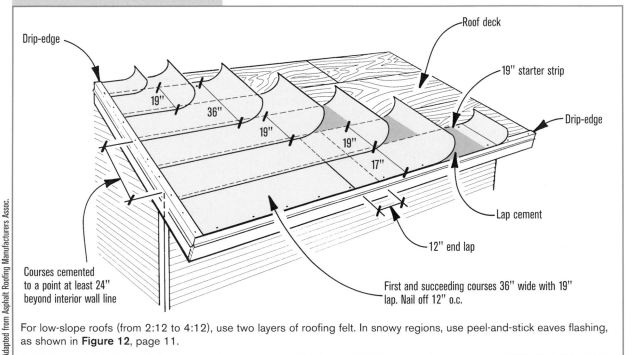

Drip-edge · Roof deck · 19" starter strip · Drip-edge · 19" · 36" · 19" · 19" · 17" · Lap cement · 12" end lap

Courses cemented to a point at least 24" beyond interior wall line

First and succeeding courses 36" wide with 19" lap. Nail off 12" o.c.

For low-slope roofs (from 2:12 to 4:12), use two layers of roofing felt. In snowy regions, use peel-and-stick eaves flashing, as shown in **Figure 12**, page 11.

Fasteners for Asphalt Shingles

Most blow-offs are caused by poorly applied, or badly chosen, fasteners.

Nails

Nails should penetrate thick plank decking by $3/4$ in. minimum; they should go all the way through thin sheathings. See **Figure 9** for proper nailing depth.

Staples

- Avoid using staples on asphalt roofs, particularly in high-wind areas; hand-driven or air-driven roofing nails are stronger.

- If you insist on using staples, adjust the staple gun so that the staple's crown rests evenly against the shingle's surface without breaking it (**Figure 9**). Any more or less, and it won't hold the shingle reliably in place.

Nailing patterns for low and normal slopes. The nailing for asphalt shingles depends on roof slope. Fasten with four nails, directly above each cutout and $1/2$ in. from each end (**Figure 10**).

Nailing pattern for steep slopes. Fasten with six nails on steep roofs, such as mansards, that slope more than 21 in. per ft.

Figure 9. Proper Nailing and Stapling

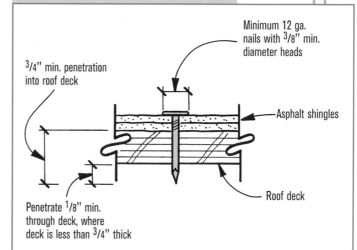

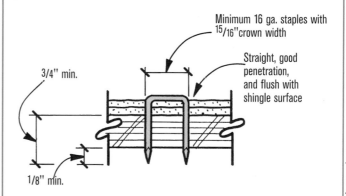

In order for fasteners to be effective, the nail head (or the crown of the staple) must bear tightly against the shingle without penetrating it. Any more or less and it will loosen over time. When reroofing over shingles, fasteners must penetrate the roof deck $3/4$ in. minimum. Use $1 1/2$- to $1 3/4$-in.-long roofing nails.

Adapted from Asphalt Roofing Manufacturers Assoc.

Seal each tab with a 1-in.-diameter dab of asphalt adhesive cement placed 2 in. above the butt at the center of each tab.

Figure 10. Nailing Patterns

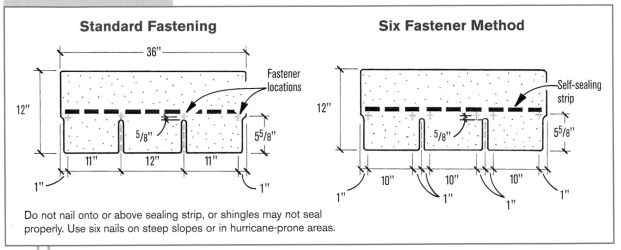

Do not nail onto or above sealing strip, or shingles may not seal properly. Use six nails on steep slopes or in hurricane-prone areas.

High winds. Use six nails per shingle in hurricane-prone areas, plus a quarter-size dab of asphalt adhesive under each tab corner (a total of six dabs).

Install shingles in warm weather so the self-sealing strip is soft enough to stick.

Shingle Installation

Starter Course

The starter course along the eaves sheds water that may migrate through the cutouts and joints of the first full shingle course.

- Use self-adhering asphalt shingles for starter courses.

- Cut off the tabs and use the remaining part of the shingle, installing it with the seal-strip along the bottom edge.

- Starter shingles should overlap the eaves and rake edges 1/4- to 3/4-in. depending on the shingle manufacturer's recommendations.

- Nail the starter strip 2$\frac{1}{2}$- to 4-in. above the overhanging edge, and 6- to 9-in. o.c.

First Full Course

Start the first course with a full shingle, and succeeding courses with varying cut lengths to produce the familiar "stair-stepped" pattern.

Stacking Bundles

Lay bundles flat on the roof; don't drape over the ridge or edges. Also distribute bundles over roof area to avoid creating concentrated loads.

Alignment Guides

Most shingles include 1/2-in. alignment slits across the top edge and half-slots along the edges. Use these to line up adjacent shingles and successive courses. In addition, shadow marks may run the length of each shingle near the top of the slots. These are meant as an aid to horizontal alignment.

Shingle Offset

How well three-tab shingles hold up over time depends to some degree on the patterns used to lay them. Although many customers prefer to see the cutouts aligned on the roof, this directs runoff into channels that erode the shingle surface.

There are four basic patterns to laying out three-tab shingles: straight-up method, half-pattern, 4-in. offset, and 5-in. offset (**Figure 11**). The 5-in.-offset pattern provides the best all-around protection.

Installation Temperature

The proper temperature range for applying asphalt shingles is 40°F to 80°F. Above or below that range they're either too brittle or too soft, and the sealing strips (or dabs of adhesive) do not seal well and can lead to blow-offs in windy areas. If installed in cool weather, however, shingles will seal when warmer air and sunlight hit them.

Low-Slope Asphalt-Shingle Roofs

You can use asphalt shingles on roofs as shallow as 2:12. However, for slopes below 4:12, most codes insist that the shingles be installed over double coverage roofing felt (**Figure 8**, page 6) with a bituminous eaves flashing.

- For low-slope roofs, use shingles that are labeled "wind-resistant," or use standard asphalt shingles and put a dab of asphalt adhesive cement beneath each tab.

- For low-slope roofs (shed dormers, for example) on sites subject to heavy wind-driven rain or heavy snow loads, cover the entire roof deck with a bituminous eaves membrane before applying shingles (**Figure 12**).

Windy Locations

In very windy locations, you can special-order wind-resistant shingles or put a dab of asphalt adhesive cement beneath each shingle tab. In hurricane-prone areas, use six nails per shingle.

Figure 11. Shingle Offset

A. Straight-Up Method

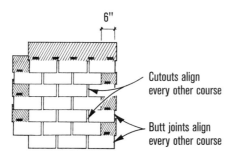

The straight-up method of laying shingles offsets alternating courses 6 in. from a vertical line up the roof (half a tab width for metric shingles). The alignment of butt joints and cutouts in every other course, however, can cause premature weathering of surface granules.

B. Half-Pattern

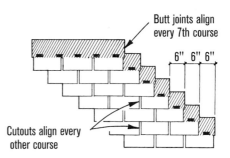

A half-pattern (also called half-tab or sixes) staggers each course with a 6-in. offset (half a tab width for metric shingles). Butt joints are better protected from water migrating horizontally, but cutouts still align every other course.

C. 4-In. Offset

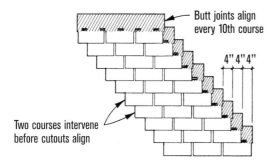

A 4-in. offset keeps cutouts separated by two courses, and butt joints align every ten courses. But the short lap doesn't provide enough protection in wet climates, or in areas with severe freeze-thaw cycles.

D. 5-In. Offset

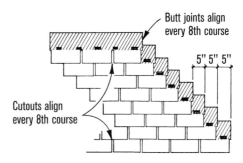

A 5-in. offset provides the best all-around protection. Both the cutouts and the butt joints align only every eight courses, so runoff is less likely to cut channels into the shingle granules. It hides shingle irregularities as well.

Reroofing

When to Strip

If more than 10% of an old roof needs repair, the best solution is usually a new roof.

Code Requirements

Most codes allow either two to three layers of asphalt or just one layer of asphalt over a layer of wood shingles. Some limit you to one layer of roofing, period. Check local code to be sure.

Incompatible Materials

The following materials just won't work together:

- **Asphalt over slate.** (Yes, it's been done.) Because of its high thermal mass, the slate acts as a heat sink. The asphalt shingles are cooked from the back. This dries them out and cuts their service life in half.

- **Asphalt over metal.** The results are the same as putting asphalt over slate, but the damage is done by radiant heat that's reflected back from the surface of the metal.

Preparing To Reroof Checklist

- Repair all leaks, damaged framing members, and any damaged or rusted flashing.

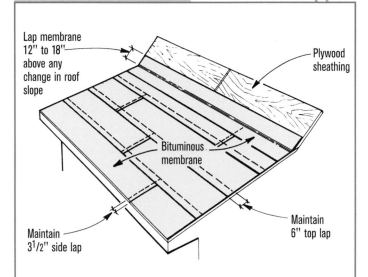

Figure 12. Waterproof Deck

Lap membrane 12" to 18" above any change in roof slope

Plywood sheathing

Bituminous membrane

Maintain 3¹/2" side lap

Maintain 6" top lap

In snowy regions, shallow slope roofs (below 2:12) and low-slope roofs (4:12 to 2:12) should be waterproofed with a peel-and-stick bituminous membrane. Laps between membrane layers should be at least 6 in. along the top edge and at least 3¹/2 in. on the sides.

- Even out the substrate by filling in any missing areas of old roofing, nail down all loose or curled shingles, and remove or drive home all loose nails.

- Install drip edge along the rakes and eaves, and eaves flashing if required.

- Over 4:12, reroofing usually doesn't require a new underlayment; the existing roof should serve the same purpose. However, some codes may require a new underlayment on shallower slopes.

Asphalt Over Asphalt

Some codes may permit three layers of asphalt, but it's usually better to have no more than two.

Do Not Use Too Many Layers

There are several reasons not to install too many layers of asphalt shingles:

- The layers may not provide adequate lateral support for nails, increasing the chance of a blow-off;
- The roof retains more heat, reducing the new shingles' life expectancy;
- The total weight might exceed the roof's design load. See **Figure 13**, to evaluate the roof structure.

Use organic-mat shingles for second layer. They're thicker than fiberglass shingles, so they won't telegraph the old roof contours as readily.

Use nails, not staples, to fasten the second layer.

Do not reroof over high-profile shingles because of theadded weight and the difficulty of producing an even surface.

Nesting Procedure for Reroofing

The nesting procedure described in **Figure 14** minimizes any unevenness that might result from installing new shingles. It also ensures that the new horizontal fastening pattern is 2 in. below the old one.

Starter Strip

- Cut the starter strip shingles wide enough to overhang the eaves and carry water into the gutter. Usually this means removing the tabs plus 2 in. from the top, so that the remaining portion is equal in width to the exposure of the old shingles (normally 5 in.).
- Apply the starter strip so that it is even with the existing roof at the eaves. Do not overlap the existing course above.
- Remove 3 in. from the rake end of the first starter strip shingle to ensure that joints between adjacent starter strip shingles will be covered when the first course is applied.

First Course

- Cut 2 in. or more from the butts of the first course of shingles so that the shingles fit between the butts of the existing third course and the eaves edge of the new starter strip.
- Start at the rake with a full-length shingle.
- Use four fasteners per shingle, locating them in the same positions as in new construction — $5/8$ in. over the cutouts and 1 in. in from the sides (**Figure 10**, page 8). Do not fasten into or above the adhesive sealing strip.

Figure 13. Maximum Rafter Span (inches) for Multiple Layers of Asphalt Shingles

		Two Layers of Shingles								Three Layers of Shingles							
Rafter Spacing		16" o.c.				24" o.c.				16" o.c.				24" o.c.			
Lumber Grade		#1	#2	#3	U	#1	#2	#3	U	#1	#2	#3	U	#1	#2	#3	U
Size	Live Load																
2x4	10 lb.	[126]	[123]	99	85	[110]	[107]	82	70	[126]	[121]	92	79	104	100	76	65
	20 lb.	[100]	[97]	80	68	[87]	[85]	65	56	[100]	[97]	76	65	86	82	62	53
	30 lb.	[87]	[85]	69	59	[76]	74	56	48	[87]	[85]	66	57	75	71	54	46
	40 lb.	[79]	[77]	61	52	69	66	50	43	[79]	[77]	59	51	67	64	49	42
	50 lb.	[74]	[72]	56	48	63	60	46	39	[74]	[71]	54	47	61	59	44	38
2x6	10 lb.	197	188	143	133	163	156	118	101	183	175	133	114	151	144	110	94
	20 lb.	[157]	152	116	99	131	125	95	82	151	145	110	94	125	119	91	78
	30 lb.	137	131	100	86	113	108	82	70	132	127	96	82	109	104	79	68
	40 lb.	122	117	89	76	100	96	73	63	119	114	86	74	97	93	71	61
	50 lb.	111	107	81	70	91	88	66	57	109	104	79	68	89	85	65	56
2x8	10 lb.	246	236	179	153	204	196	148	127	229	219	166	143	190	182	138	118
	20 lb.	200	191	145	125	165	158	120	103	190	182	138	119	157	150	114	98
	30 lb.	173	165	125	108	142	136	103	89	166	159	121	104	137	131	99	85
	40 lb.	154	148	112	96	127	121	92	79	150	143	109	93	123	118	89	77
	50 lb.	141	135	102	88	115	111	84	72	137	131	100	86	113	108	82	70
2x10	10 lb.	296	284	215	185	247	237	180	154	276	265	201	172	230	220	167	143
	20 lb.	242	232	176	151	200	192	146	125	231	221	168	144	191	183	139	119
	30 lb.	209	201	152	131	173	165	126	108	202	193	147	126	167	159	121	104
	40 lb.	187	179	136	117	154	148	112	96	182	174	132	113	150	143	109	93
	50 lb.	171	164	124	107	141	135	102	88	167	160	121	104	137	131	100	86
2x12	10 lb.	339	325	246	212	284	272	206	177	317	303	230	198	264	253	192	165
	20 lb.	278	266	202	173	231	221	168	144	265	254	193	165	220	211	160	137
	30 lb.	241	231	175	150	200	191	145	124	233	223	169	145	192	184	140	120
	40 lb.	216	207	157	135	178	171	129	111	210	201	153	131	173	166	126	108
	50 lb.	197	189	143	123	163	156	118	101	193	185	140	120	159	152	115	99

Notes: Chart assumes asphalt shingles @ 3 psf per layer, plywood @ 1.5 psf, L/240 deflection. Rafter spans in brackets [ ] are controlled by deflection.

To use the chart, go down the left-hand column to the correct row for the rafter size and snow load for your area. Move across the chart to the correct rafter spacing and lumber grade to find the maximum length that the rafters can span. The chart is based on Douglas fir grades 1, 2, and 3. In cases where no grade stamp is available, use the "U" column for unknown species. Span is measured horizontally, not on the slope. This chart is not applicable to cathedral ceilings, which have ceiling materials attached to rafters.

Second and Succeeding Courses

- Use full-width shingles.

- Remove 6 in. from the rake end of the first shingle in each succeeding course, through the sixth.

- Place the top edge of the new shingles against the butt edge of the old shingles in the course above.

- Repeat the cycle by starting the seventh course with a full-length shingle.

Figure 14. Reroofing Using the Nesting Procedure

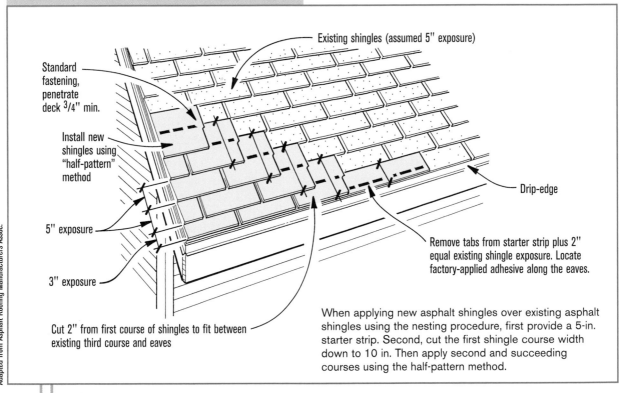

Existing shingles (assumed 5" exposure)

Standard fastening, penetrate deck 3/4" min.

Install new shingles using "half-pattern" method

Drip-edge

5" exposure

3" exposure

Remove tabs from starter strip plus 2" equal existing shingle exposure. Locate factory-applied adhesive along the eaves.

Cut 2" from first course of shingles to fit between existing third course and eaves

When applying new asphalt shingles over existing asphalt shingles using the nesting procedure, first provide a 5-in. starter strip. Second, cut the first shingle course width down to 10 in. Then apply second and succeeding courses using the half-pattern method.

Wood Shingles and Shakes

Grades and Types

Wood shingles are sawn on both sides to produce a smooth, uniform surface. Shakes, on the other hand, are split from logs, leaving both sides rough (see **Figure 15** for both shake and shingle types).

Lengths and Weights

Shingles come in three lengths: 16-in. (sometimes called 5X), 18-in. (perfections), and 24-in. (royals). See **Figure 16** for specification information.

Shakes come in 18- and 24-in. lengths, as well as in a 15-in.-long starter/finish shake. They're available in two weights: mediums have $1/2$-in. butts; heavies have $3/4$-in. butts on average.

Figure 15. Types of Wood Shingles and Shakes

No. 1 Blue Label®
The premium grade of shingles for roofs and sidewalls. These top-grade shingles are 100% heartwood, 100% clear, and 100% edge-grain.

No. 2 Red Label
A good grade for many applications. Not less than 10" clear on 16" shingles, 11" clear on 18" shingles, and 16" clear on 24" shingles. Flat grain and limited sapwood are permitted in this grade.

No. 3 Black Label
A utility grade for economy applications and secondary buildings. Not less than 6" clear on 16" and 18" shingles, 10" clear on 24" shingles.

No. 4 Undercoursing
A utility grade for starter course undercoursing.

No. 1 Hand-split & Resawn
These shakes have split faces and sawn backs. Cedar logs are first cut into desired lengths. Blanks or boards of proper thickness are split and then run diagonally through a bandsaw to produce two tapered shakes from each blank.

No. 1 Certi-Sawn®
These shakes are sawn both sides. No. 2 and 3 are also available.

No. 1 Tapersplit
Produced largely by hand, using a sharp-bladed steel froe and a mallet. The natural shingle-like taper is achieved by reversing the block, end-for-end, with each split.

No. 1 Straightsplit
Produced by machine or in the same manner as tapersplit shakes except they are split from the same end of the block, so the shakes have the same thickness throughout.

Adapted from Cedar Shake and Shingle Bureau

Figure 16. Typical Wood Shingles and Shakes

Shingles

Grade	Length	Exposure 3:12 to 4:12	Exposure 4:12 & beyond	Courses per Bundle	Bundles per Square
No. 1	16"[1]	$3^3/4$"	5"	20/20	4 bundles
Blue Label	18"[2]	$4^1/4$"	$5^1/2$"	18/18	4 bundles
No. 2	24"[3]	$5^3/4$"	$7^1/2$"	13/14	4 bundles
Red Label	16"[1]	$3^1/2$"	4"	20/20	4 bundles
	18"[2]	4"	$4^1/2$"	18/18	4 bundles
	24"[3]	$5^1/2$"	$6^1/2$"	13/14	4 bundles
No. 3	16"[1]	3"	$3^1/2$"	20/20	4 bundles
Black	18"[2]	$3^1/2$"	4"	18/18	4 bundles
Label	24"[3]	5"	$5^1/2$"	13/14	4 bundles
No. 4	16"	N/A	N/A	14/14 or 20/20	2 bundles
Undercoursing	18"	N/A	N/A	14/14 or 18/18	2 bundles
No. 1 or No. 2	16"[1]	$3^3/4$"	5"	33/33	1 carton
Rebutted/	18"[2]	$4^1/4$"	$5^1/2$"	28/28	1 carton
Rejointed	24"[3]	$5^3/4$"	$7^1/2$"	13/14	4 bundles

(1) 5X; (2) perfections; (3) royals
Slope – 4:12 to 12:12 is normal. 3:12 is considered minimum. For 3:12 to 4:12, reduce exposure (see exposure column). Below 3:12, create a waterproof deck (see **Figure 12**, page 11).
Life Expectancy – 8 to 25 years (See note at right regarding life expectancy.)

Shakes

Grade	Length & Thickness	Maximum Exposure (4:12 & steeper)	Courses per Bundle	Bundles per Square
			18" pack*	
No. 1	15" starter-finish	$7^1/2$" (for 18")	9/9	5
Hand-split	18" x $1/2$" to $3/4$"		9/9	5
& Resawn	18" x $3/4$" to $1^1/4$"		9/9	5
	24" x $3/8$"*	10" (for 24")	9/9	5
	24" x $1/2$" to $3/4$"		9/9	5
	24" x $3/4$" to $1^1/4$"		9/9	5
No. 1	24" x $1/2$" to $5/8$"	10"	9/9	5
Tapersplit				
			20" pack	
No. 1	18" x $3/8$" *	$7^1/2$"	14 straight	4
Straight-	18" x $3/8$"	$7^1/2$"	19 straight	5
split	24" x $3/8$"	10"	16 straight	5

*True-edge (24 x $3/8$" hand-split shakes limited to 5" maximum weather exposure, per U.B.C.)
Slope – 4:12 to 12:12 is normal. Below 4:12, create a waterproof deck (see **Figure 12**, page 11).
Life Expectancy – 10 to 30 years
Note: Wood can be broken down by excessive moisture as well as by moss and other fungi, both of which are more common on north-facing surfaces. In the absence of moisture problems, however, the south side of a roof tends to degrade quicker because of its higher temperature and increased UV exposure. You can get a 30-year warranty if shingles or shakes have been pressure-treated at the factory.

Exposures and Slope

Normal-exposure shingles and shakes can be used on slopes as low as 4:12.

Low Slopes

- For roofs from 3:12 to 4:12, you can use shingles if you reduce the exposure as noted in **Figure 16**.

- For slopes lower than 3:12 (4:12 for shakes), you need to first create a waterproof deck, then lay vertical strapping up the roof with spaced sheathing over it (**Figure 20**, page

20). The wood roof on top, in this case, is purely decorative.

Snowy Regions

Use a double layer of felt (preferably cemented together) at the eaves, or a bituminous eaves flashing (see "Eaves Flashing," page 73).

Fire Retardants

Fire-Rated Materials

The only shingles with permanent fire-resistance are pressure-treated at the factory and carry the Cedar Shake and Shingle Bureau's Certi-Guard label.

Certi-Guard shingles are available with a Class-B or Class-C fire rating at about twice the price of untreated shingles.

Field-applied fire retardants give protection for six months to one year at most. You can get comparable results from treating with a high-phosphate fertilizer, which is inexpensive and non-corrosive to flashings. Phosphates give a Class-C fire rating for about six months (they'll take up to 30 in. of rainfall before losing their fire resistance). Re-apply every spring and fall.

Underlayment

A permeable 15-lb or 30-lb felt is typically installed only over the solid sheathing area at eaves (**Figure 17**).

Sheathing Options for Shingles

It is best to install wood roofing over spaced sheathing — evenly spaced 1x4s or 1x6s (**Figure 18**). Shingles installed on solid sheathing can't dry out as well. Because their back sides stay wet while the sun beats on their face, they decay faster and are more likely to cup, curl, and split.

Figure 17. Sheathing and Underlayment for Wood Roofs

	Sheathing	Interlayment	Underlayment[1]
Wood Shingles	Spaced[3]	none	15-lb or 30-lb felt over section of solid sheathing at eaves
	Solid[2 & 4]	none	15-lb or 30-lb felt at eaves. Optional over field of roof
Wood Shakes	Spaced[3]	30-lb asphalt-saturated felt	30-lb felt over section of solid sheathing at eaves
	Solid[2 & 4]	30-lb asphalt-saturated felt	30-lb felt at eaves

(1) Underlayment at eaves should extend to a point 12–24 in. inside building. Bituminous eaves flashing recommended in cold, snowy climates.
(2) Use to protect against windblown snow or where required for structural reasons. May shorten life of shingles and shakes.
(3) Recommended in hot, humid climates.
(4) Cedar Breather® is recommended to provide ventilation between underlayment and shingles.

Spaced Sheathing

- One option is to space 1x4s to coincide with the weather exposure of the shingles as shown in **Figure 19**.

- The other option is to use 1x6s such that two courses of shingles are nailed to each 1x6, as shown in **Figure 18**.

Solid Sheathing

Solid sheathing is required for wood shingles only for structural reasons — such as in seismic zones — or for protection against wind-blown snow. If the job demands solid sheathing, strap the roof or use a ventilating underlayment, as follows:

Strapping Over Plywood

- Sheathe the roof deck with plywood;

- Cover the plywood with 15- or 30-lb. asphalt-impregnated felt paper;

- Install horizontal 1x3 strapping over the plywood, cutting $^1/2$-in. notches at 4 ft. o.c. on the bottom of the strapping for drainage;

- Install the shingles over the strapping, following the installation details for spaced sheathing. An alternative to notching is to lay vertical strapping first, and then horizontal strapping.

Figure 18. Shingle Installation

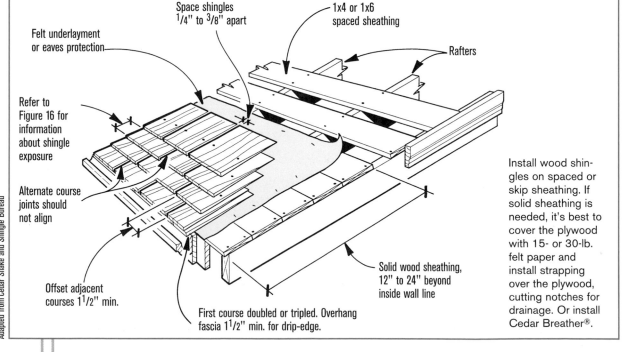

Felt underlayment or eaves protection

Space shingles $^1/4$" to $^3/8$" apart

1x4 or 1x6 spaced sheathing

Rafters

Refer to Figure 16 for information about shingle exposure

Alternate course joints should not align

Offset adjacent courses $1^1/2$" min.

First course doubled or tripled. Overhang fascia $1^1/2$" min. for drip-edge.

Solid wood sheathing, 12" to 24" beyond inside wall line

Install wood shingles on spaced or skip sheathing. If solid sheathing is needed, it's best to cover the plywood with 15- or 30-lb. felt paper and install strapping over the plywood, cutting notches for drainage. Or install Cedar Breather®.

Adapted from Cedar Shake and Shingle Bureau

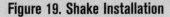

Figure 19. Shake Installation

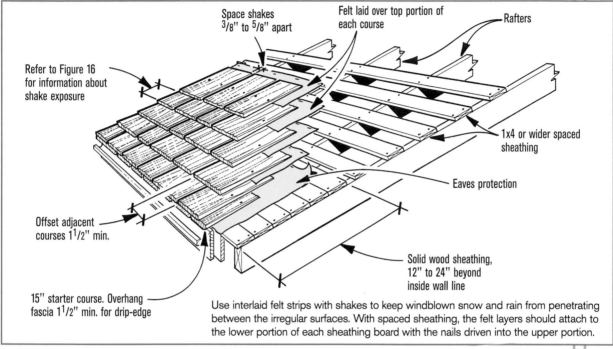

Space shakes ³/₈" to ⁵/₈" apart

Felt laid over top portion of each course

Rafters

Refer to Figure 16 for information about shake exposure

1x4 or wider spaced sheathing

Eaves protection

Offset adjacent courses 1¹/₂" min.

Solid wood sheathing, 12" to 24" beyond inside wall line

15" starter course. Overhang fascia 1¹/₂" min. for drip-edge

Use interlaid felt strips with shakes to keep windblown snow and rain from penetrating between the irregular surfaces. With spaced sheathing, the felt layers should attach to the lower portion of each sheathing board with the nails driven into the upper portion.

Adapted from Cedar Shake and Shingle Bureau

Ventilating Underlayment

Another option for ventilating shingles installed over plywood is a product called Cedar Breather® (Benjamin Obdyke, Horsham, Pa., www.obdyke.com). The ³/₈-in.-thick material comes in 39-in.-wide rolls. Its matrix of synthetic fibers is stiff enough to resist crushing, so it provides continuous airflow between the roof deck and the wood roofing.

• Install Cedar Breather® course by course just ahead of the shingles, tacking it in place with 5d galvanized box nails.

• The seams are butted (not overlapped) and can be cut easily with shears.

Sheathing Options for Shakes

Because the irregular surface of hand-split shakes makes them somewhat self-ventilating, they may be installed over either spaced or solid sheathing in most cases.

Spaced sheathing for shakes is a must in hot, humid regions, however, because the shakes need a greater drying potential. For shakes, spaced sheathing usually consists of 1x6s spaced on centers equal to the weather exposure of the shakes.

Solid sheathing for shakes is preferable in three instances: on roofs with slopes of less than 4:12; in snowy regions where windblown snow could penetrate the shakes; and in earthquake-prone regions where the sheathing must act as a shear diaphragm.

Interlayment for Shake Roofs

Because of the rough profile, each course of cedar shakes must be laid over an 18-in.-wide interlayment of 30-lb. felt. The felt serves as a baffle against wind-driven snow and rain (**Figure 19**).

Install interlayment by fastening the strips to the sheathing, then apply the shakes by slipping their top edges under the felt interlayment strips.

Interlayment Layout

- The first strip of interlayment protects the eaves overhang, so its bottom edge should be twice the distance from the eaves edge as the weather exposure you plan to use.

- The second strip starts two exposure widths up from the bottom edge of the roof.

- Install the remaining strips on centers that equal the weather exposure. Make sure the top edge of each layer of felt rests on a section of sheathing, or it won't provide a good baffle.

Underlayment on Shallow Roofs

The Council of American Building Officials (CABO) sets a minimum

Figure 20. Low-Slope Shingle and Shake Installation

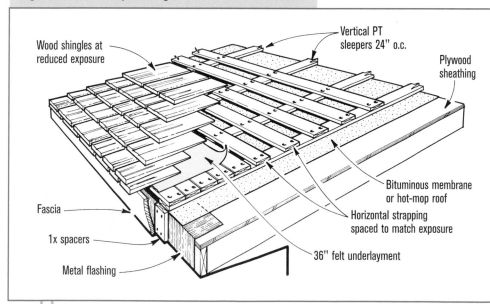

Wood shingles at reduced exposure

Vertical PT sleepers 24" o.c.

Plywood sheathing

Bituminous membrane or hot-mop roof

Horizontal strapping spaced to match exposure

Fascia

1x spacers

Metal flashing

36" felt underlayment

On shallow slopes, install wood shingles and shakes over a watertight subroof and a framework of pressure-treated strapping. The fascia is spaced out from the metal flashing at the eaves to allow any water that gets under the roofing to drain from the subroof.

slope of 3:12 for wood shingles and 4:12 for shakes. For lower slopes, NRCA and the Cedar Shake and Shingle Bureau recommend installing wood roofing on a lattice-like framework of pressure-treated strapping over a watertight membrane (**Figure 20**).

Fasteners for Shingles and Shakes

Shingles and shakes can be fastened with nails or staples, as follows:

Nails

- Use only corrosion-resistant, hot-dipped galvanized, stainless-steel, or aluminum nails.

- For hip and ridge caps, use nails two sizes larger than in the field (**Figure 21**).

- Drive nails so they rest on the surface of the wood. Nails that crush the surface will encourage the shingle to split (**Figure 22**).

- Wide shakes and shingles will eventually split. To avoid problems, make a vertical score down its center with a utility knife and drive a nail on either side of the score. Treat the score as a joint, offsetting it at least $1^1/2$ in. from any joints directly above or below.

- Refer to **Figure 23** for nailing patterns.

Figure 21. Nails for Shingles and Shakes

Shingles	Nail Type	Minimum Length
16" and 18"	3d box	$1^1/4"$
24"	4d box	$1^1/2"$
Shakes		
18" Straight-Split	5d box	$1^3/4"$
18" and 24" Hand-split-and-Resawn	6d box	2"
24" Tapersplit	5d box	$1^3/4"$
18" and 24" Taper-sawn	6d box	2"

Adapted from Cedar Shake and Shingle Bureau

Figure 22. Nailing Depths

Incorrect   Correct

Nails should rest on the surface of the wood. If the nailheads crush the wood fibers, movement will be limited and the shingle will be more apt to split.

Staples

- Use only aluminum or Types 304 or 316 stainless-steel fasteners. Galvanized staples on wood roofs will rust.

- When using a pneumatic nailer, it's important to adjust it so that the staples don't tear the wood fibers, as this will reduce their holding power.

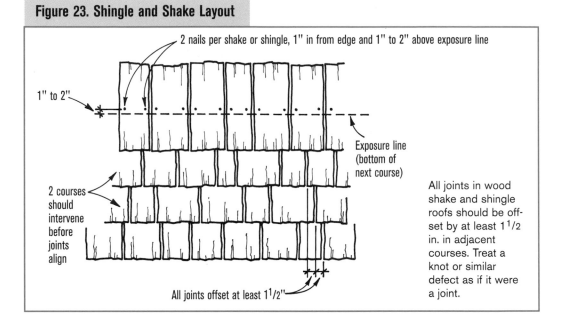

Figure 23. Shingle and Shake Layout

2 nails per shake or shingle, 1" in from edge and 1" to 2" above exposure line

1" to 2"

Exposure line (bottom of next course)

2 courses should intervene before joints align

All joints in wood shake and shingle roofs should be off-set by at least 1 1/2 in. in adjacent courses. Treat a knot or similar defect as if it were a joint.

All joints offset at least 1 1/2"

Installing Shingles and Shakes

Keyway

Like all wooden materials, shingles and shakes swell when wet. To compensate, make a "keyway" by separating shingles by 1/4 in. to 3/8 in. (about the width of a pencil), or by separating shakes 3/8 in. to 5/8 in. This keyway can be omitted when working with wet shingles, since they'll shrink rather than expand.

Rake Treatment

To eliminate dripping water at gable end walls, nail a clapboard along each rake under the shingles or shakes. The flair will direct water toward the center of the roof.

Ridges and Hips

- Cap ridges and hips to ensure a weathertight joint.

- Use either premanufactured ridge and hip caps (sold in bundles) or assemble them on site. Either type must have alternate overlaps and concealed nailing.

- Weather exposures should be the same as for shingles or shakes in the field of the roof.

- Nails must penetrate 3/4 in. into the sheathing or completely pass through it (**Figure 24**).

Vented Ridges

To vent wood shingle roofs, hold the plywood sheathing back at the ridge, leaving a 1-in. gap (**Figure 25**).

- After the roof shingles are installed, cover the ridge with a synthetic matrix material such as Roll Vent® (Benjamin Obdyke, Horsham, Pa., www.obdyke.com).

- Center matrix over the ridge, tack it in place, and then cover it with a 7-in.-wide strip of 30-lb. felt.

- When the Roll Vent® is in place, cap the ridge with manufactured cedar ridge caps.

- Attach the ridge caps using 2-in.-long ¹/₂-in.-crown galvanized staples. Use a staple gun, as hand-nailing the ridge caps through the mushy Roll Vent® material will result in excessive splitting of the cap shingles.

Maintenance and Repair

Shingles and shakes need more care than other types of roofs. Fungus and rot are very much at home on wood roofs, particularly low-pitched roofs in humid, wooded areas. Parts of the roof beneath overhanging trees are especially vulnerable since wet debris such as needles and leaves can trap moisture, leading to fungus growth, premature rot, and leaks.

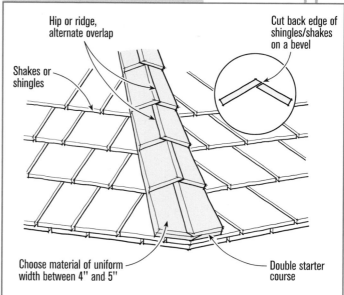

Figure 24. Hip and Ridge Details

Hip or ridge, alternate overlap

Cut back edge of shingles/shakes on a bevel

Shakes or shingles

Choose material of uniform width between 4" and 5"

Double starter course

Alternate overlaps and conceal nailing at ridges and hips to provide a weathertight joint. Use nails long enough to penetrate the sheathing ³/4 in. minimum. Factory-assembled ridge and hip units are available. They come with shingles ganged together for ease of installation.

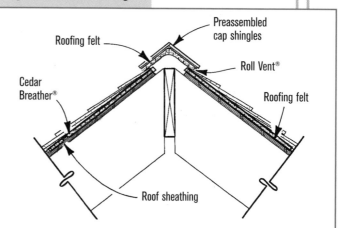

Figure 25. Vented Ridge

Roofing felt

Preassembled cap shingles

Roll Vent®

Cedar Breather®

Roofing felt

Roof sheathing

A vented ridge can be created using Roll Vent®, 30-lb. felt paper, and preassembled ridge cap shingles. Install with a pneumatic staple gun to prevent splitting.

Cleaning a Wood Roof

Cleaning with a power washer or garden sprayer can double a wood roof's service life. Clean roofs yearly, paying particular attention to the keyways between adjacent shingles.

- A high-pressure water sprayer works best. Use a power washer with a flow rate of 4 to 6 gallons per minute.

- Or use a 50/50 solution of water and household bleach (for an even stronger solution, replace the bleach with 2 to 4 ounces of swimming-pool chlorine) in a garden pump. Spray 1 to 1½ gallons of this solution over each square of roof area. Let it stand for 15 to 30 minutes, and then rinse it off with a power washer or garden hose.

- Protect the surrounding shrubs and grass: Hose them down with clean water before, during, and after application, or cover them with tarps.

Minor Repairs

Cracked Shingles

- If both sides of a cracked shingle are still present, nail them to the roof deck.

- Drill pilot holes first to prevent splitting the shingle and cover both the joint and the nail heads with roofing cement.

Temporary Repair

- A damaged shingle can be temporarily repaired by inserting a piece of galvanized steel or aluminum under it and nailing through the shingle and metal with two nails.

- The metal should extend 2 in. beyond both edges of the shingle and 1 in. under the butt line of the overlying shingle in the next course.

Shingle Replacement

- Individual shingles can be removed by first splitting them and removing the pieces. Cut the roofing nails with a shingle ripper or hacksaw blade. Make sure that the nails are cut off flush with the sheathing; use caution when cutting the nails to avoid damage to the roof deck sheathing or underlayment.

- Next, trim the replacement shingle to the required width and slide it into place. Tap it gently into place with a hammer and wood block. Nail it to the roof deck and cover the nail heads with roofing cement.

Bowed Shingles

- Split a bowed shingle down the center and remove about $1/4$ in. of wood from the inside edge of one section to form a joint for roofing cement.

- Nail the two sections on either side of the joint and cover the joint and nail heads with roofing cement.

Reroofing

When to Strip

As with asphalt shingles, if more than 10% of an old roof needs repair, the best solution is usually a new roof. Avoid roofing over wet or water-damaged wood shingles and wood shakes; they're too irregular to make a good base.

Slate

New slate is not installed much these days, so this section focuses on inspection and repair.

Working on Slate

When working on existing slates, never walk directly on the roof surface. Dry slates are slippery; wet ones are as slick as ice. All slates are brittle and easily broken.

- If you must walk on the roof, spread your weight with foam insulation or plywood underfoot. Walk in the valleys, or hook a ladder over the ridge and rest it on some sort of cushion (a double layer of batt insulation will do).

- If the nails look very rusty, use extreme caution: when walked on, they could come loose.

Inspecting Slates

If possible, inspect the roof from the attic.

Evaluate Slate Conditions

The natural weathering of slates slowly chips and flakes off paper-thin laminations. Also, slates become soft and spongy as the inner layers begin to delaminate. Old, weathered slates tend to hold more moisture than new slates. This leads to further deterioration and even rot in the roof sheathing underneath.

Figure 26. Sizing Replacement Slate

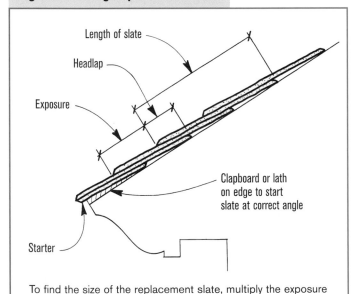

Length of slate

Headlap

Exposure

Clapboard or lath
on edge to start
slate at correct angle

Starter

To find the size of the replacement slate, multiply the exposure by 2, and add 3 in. for the headlap. Round up to 12-, 14-, or 16-in.

Figure 27. Replacing Damaged Slate

(1) To remove the damaged slate, first hook the ripper on one of the two nails holding the slate. (2) Then hammer downward on the ripper to cut or pull the nail. (3) Next, nail a new slate into place with one nail and slide in a piece of copper flashing to cover the nail hole. Or hang the slate from a slate hook (**Figure 28**) or copper nail.

Inspect Nails

The tips of nails can give a good indication of their condition. On the roof surface, signs of deteriorated nails include loose slates or a large number of repairs.

Inspect Transitions

When inspecting a slate roof, look closely at ridges, valleys, dormers, and other changes in roof direction. Cracked slates around a valley are a tipoff that something is trapping water. When the water freezes, it cracks the slate above it. Also look for roof cement — it's a sign of improper maintenance.

Moss and Mineral Deposits

Excessive moss and mildew are as harmful to slates as to other roof coverings. Moss traps moisture and its roots can penetrate and damage the slate. High moisture levels in the attic can also cause deterioration. Look for mineral deposits on the top or bottom surface of the slates, which indicate such underlying moisture problems and result in shortened shingle life.

Finding Leaks

In a severe windblown rain, even a good slate roof may get an occasional leak. Such leaks show up at inside corners, near valleys, and around chimneys. They're most common on shallow roofs.

Nail Holes

If an otherwise sound and well-designed roof leaks during a long rainstorm, look for nail holes that were punched too low or too close to the slates' centers. They may be letting water seep in from the end laps.

Figure 28. Installing a Slate Hook

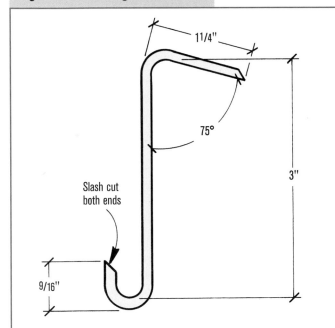

A slate hook is driven into the sheathing in the joint under the replacement slate. Use copper or stainless steel for a permanent replacement repair.

Slate Repair Checklist

Replacing a few broken slates is a simple procedure, but it must be done carefully or you can end up breaking more slates.

Measure Slates

To find the length required for a replacement slate, you can sometimes measure an exposed side at a gable end or valley. Another way is to multiply the exposure by 2 and add 3 in. as shown in **Figure 26**, page 26.

Remove Damaged Slate

To remove a damaged slate, slide a slate ripper beneath it and hook onto one of the nails. Taking care not to put any upward pressure on the ripper (you don't want to crack any undamaged slates), hammer down on it until you either cut the nail or pull it out. Repeat for any other nails.

Install Replacement

The traditional technique is to nail punch or drill one hole in the replacement slate to line up with the joint between the two slates above. Nail in the joint with a copper nail, with the head trimmed if necessary. Then slide a 3x8-in. piece of copper flashing in place to cover the nail hole (**Figure 27**, page 27).

Nailing

Most slate roof failures are caused by improper nailing or by corroded nails or flashings. Galvanized nails, for example, may wear out long before the slates. For best results, use copper flashings and 14-gauge copper nails. They're expensive, but they'll last the life of the roof.

Nails should be set lightly so slates hang freely from the nails. Nails driven too far will crack the slate. Underdriven nails will crack the slate above.

Slate Hook

Another method is to fasten a copper or stainless-steel slate hook (available from most slate suppliers) in the joint beneath the slate you're replacing, as shown in **Figure 28**. Drive the hook's 3-in. shaft into the roof sheathing above the headlap of the slate below it.

Then slide the new slate into place and pull it down until it rests in the bend of the hook.

In mild climates where snow and ice are not a problem, a strip of copper flashing bent to hold the slate can be used instead of a slate hook.

Cutting Slate

For a small number of cuts, a carborundum blade on a circular saw will do. When cutting a lot of slates, use a power tile saw or snap cutter.

Punching Nail Holes

To make nail holes, drill with carbide, or punch a hole (from the back of the slate) using the sharp point on a slater's hammer.

Clay and Concrete Tile

Roofing tile typically means clay or concrete tile (**Figure 29**). A good tile roof should include a 50-year warranty and can last over a century. When properly installed, most come with a Class-A fire rating.

Weight of Roofing Tile

A tile roof can weigh three to five times as much as an asphalt one (900 to 1,000 pounds per square is typical, although you can get lightweight Portland cement and mineral-fiber tiles that weigh only 400 to 800 pounds per square). This means tile roofs impose three to five times the design dead loads on the roof structure. Be sure to evaluate the framing before applying tile.

When installing tile, make sure to stack the tile properly to avoid overloading the roof (see "Loading the Roof with Tile," **page 43**).

Slope Limitations of Roofing Tile

With tile, as with slate, the steeper the roof the better.

- The minimum recommended slope for a concrete one-piece barrel tile or interlocking flat-ribbed tile is 4:12.

- For flat tile, the minimum slope should be 5:12.

- Code prohibits the installation of any concrete tile on slopes less than 3:12, except with permission of the building official.

Clay Tile

Clay is porous, but when tiles are fired in a kiln at about 2,000°F, the individual particles fuse together and eventually "vitrify," forming a waterproof glaze at the surface. Tile with substantially damaged edges or surfaces should be discarded.

Figure 29. Typical Clay & Concrete Tile

	Types	Min. Slope	Overall Length x Width	Exposure Length x Width	Approx. Weight/ Square	Approx. Pieces/ Square
Clay — Pan & Cover	Tapered or straight mission, barrel or barrel mission: overlapping	4:12	16" x 8"	13$\frac{1}{2}$" x 5$\frac{3}{4}$"	1,115 lbs.	192
			19" x 10"	16" x 13$\frac{1}{2}$"	1,005 lbs.	134
			18" x 12"	14" x 9$\frac{1}{2}$"	1,040 lbs.	108
	Spanish or "S"	4:12	13$\frac{1}{4}$" x 9$\frac{3}{4}$"	10$\frac{1}{4}$" x 8$\frac{1}{4}$"	900 lbs.	171
			12" x 12"	10$\frac{1}{2}$" x 9$\frac{1}{2}$"	900 lbs.	144
			17" x 13$\frac{1}{2}$"	14" x 12"	950 lbs.	92
			20" x 13$\frac{1}{4}$"	17" x 11$\frac{3}{8}$"	1,100 lbs.	75
Flat Tile	English shingle, closed shingle, or French: interlocking	3:12	11" x 8$\frac{3}{4}$"	8" x 8"	900 lbs.	225
			14" x 9"	11" x 8$\frac{1}{4}$"	800 lbs.	158
			16$\frac{1}{2}$" x 13"	13$\frac{1}{2}$" x 11$\frac{3}{4}$"	900 lbs.	90
	Plain tile, English flat or slab shingle: overlapping	4:12	12" x 7"	5" x 7"	1,840 lbs.	412
			15" x 7"	6$\frac{1}{2}$" x 7"	1,600 lbs.	31
			18" x 8"	7$\frac{1}{2}$" x 8"	1,200 lbs.	240
Concrete	High-Profile: interlocking	4:12	17" x 12$\frac{3}{8}$"	14" x 10$\frac{3}{4}$"	950 lbs.	94
	Low-Profile: interlocking	4:12	16$\frac{1}{2}$" x 13"	13$\frac{1}{2}$" x 11$\frac{3}{4}$"	900 lbs.	90
	Flat Tile: interlocking	4:12	11" x 8$\frac{3}{4}$"	8" x 8"	1,000 lbs.	225

Clay Tile Styles

There are two categories of clay tile (**Figure 30**):

- **Pan and cover tile** includes two-piece (Barrel or Mission, Roman and Greek) or one-piece (Spanish or "S").

- **Flat tile**, such as English flat, or "scab," or French "flat ribbed" tile, typically have interlocking edges.

Most manufacturers make ridge, hip, and rake tile to match both styles of clay tile. In either style, tiles may interlock with one another or overlap.

Clay Tile Color

The color of the tile is determined by the color of the clay. Most are natural earth tones: tan, reddish brown, and orange. A range of additional colors made with metallic glazes and paints may also be available.

Figure 30. Types of Clay Tile

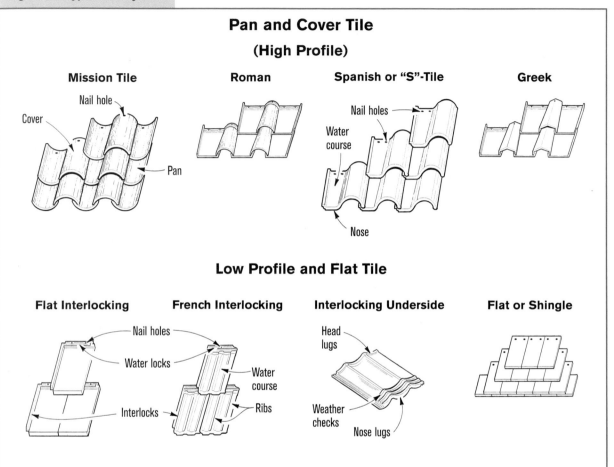

Pan and Cover Tile

(High Profile)

Mission Tile **Roman** **Spanish or "S"-Tile** **Greek**

Cover

Nail hole

Pan

Nail holes

Water course

Nose

Low Profile and Flat Tile

Flat Interlocking **French Interlocking** **Interlocking Underside** **Flat or Shingle**

Nail holes

Water locks

Interlocks

Water course

Ribs

Head lugs

Weather checks

Nose lugs

Freeze-Thaw Protection

In regions with frequent freeze-thaw cycles, use tiles that have been fired to full vitrification, giving them a glass-like surface. To resist damage from ice, these tiles need an absorption rate of less than 3% and a compressive strength of at least 8,000 psi.

Concrete Tile

Concrete tiles are made from sand and Portland cement in a 3:1 or 4:1 ratio that's extruded under high pressure, making them impermeable to water. Each has an interlocking channel on its left edge that's lapped by the next tile. On the underside, a head lug fits

Figure 31. Types of Concrete Tile

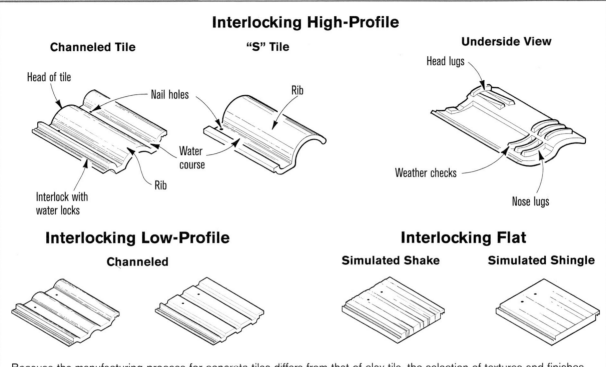

Interlocking High-Profile

Channeled Tile

"S" Tile

Underside View

Head of tile

Nail holes

Rib

Head lugs

Water course

Rib

Weather checks

Interlock with water locks

Nose lugs

Interlocking Low-Profile

Channeled

Interlocking Flat

Simulated Shake

Simulated Shingle

Because the manufacturing process for concrete tiles differs from that of clay tile, the selection of textures and finishes is more varied.

snugly over the edge of a 1x batten. A series of ridges called weather checks rest on the tile below and act as a barrier against windblown rain.

Concrete Tile Styles

Concrete tiles fall into three main categories (**Figure 31**):

- **High-profile** styles imitate traditional clay tiles (Mission, Spanish, Barrel, or S tiles).

- **Low-profile** tiles have less pronounced curves, but still have water

channels running down the face of each tile.

- **Flat tiles** imitate shakes or slate, and are laid with a staggered bond (each joint is offset from the courses above and below). Flat tiles are a little easier to fudge when trying to keep courses straight than high- or low-profile tiles. And unlike profiled tiles, they don't leave big voids at rakes, hips, and ridges that have to be sealed up with mortar.

Figure 32. Underlayment for Tile Roofs

Roof Slope	Use Conditions	Underlayment (based on standard size tile with 3" min. overlap)
More than 20:12 slope	Normal conditions	One layer of 30-lb asphalt-saturated felt (min).
	Heavier/Thicker tile application	One layer of 40-lb A-S, coated felt. Check with tile manufacturer if heavier felt is required.
	In areas with severe weather	Two layers of 30-lb A-S felt or one layer of 40-lb (A-S, coated felt) recommended.
8:12 to 20:12 slope	Normal conditions	Two layers of 30-lb A-S felt recommended, but one layer of 40-lb (A-S, coated felt) recommended.
	Heavier/Thicker tile application	One layer of 45-lb min. A-S, coated felt. Check with tile manufacturer if heavier felt is required.
	In areas with severe weather	Two layers of 30-lb A-S felt or one layer of 40-lb A-S coated felt acceptable.
4:12 to 8:12 slope	Normal conditions	Two layers of 30-lb A-S felt or one layer of 40-lb A-S coated felt recommended.
	Heavier/Thicker tile application	One layer of 45-lb min. A-S, coated felt. Check with tile manufacturer if heavier felt is required.
	In areas with severe weather	On lower slopes an upgraded underlayment system and/or waterproof membrane is recommended. Check with the manufacturer and local building officials.
Less than 4:12 slope	All conditions	At these slopes, tile is considered decorative. A more stringent underlayment, waterproof membrane system, and reduced tile exposures may be required. Check with tile manufacturer and local building officials.

Figure 33. Underlayment and Batten Layout

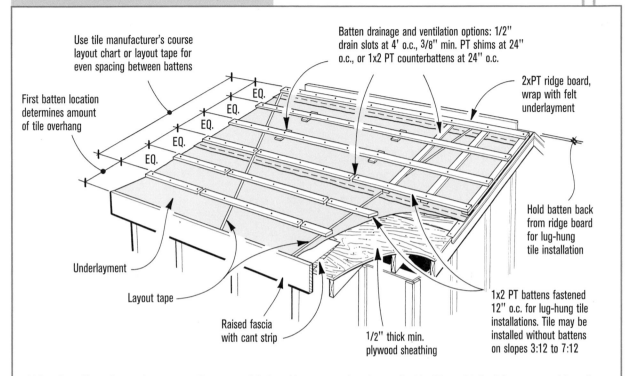

Use tile manufacturer's course layout chart or layout tape for even spacing between battens

Batten drainage and ventilation options: 1/2" drain slots at 4' o.c., 3/8" min. PT shims at 24" o.c., or 1x2 PT counterbattens at 24" o.c.

2xPT ridge board, wrap with felt underlayment

First batten location determines amount of tile overhang

EQ.
EQ.
EQ.
EQ.
EQ.

Hold batten back from ridge board for lug-hung tile installation

Underlayment

Layout tape

Raised fascia with cant strip

1/2" thick min. plywood sheathing

1x2 PT battens fastened 12" o.c. for lug-hung tile installations. Tile may be installed without battens on slopes 3:12 to 7:12

When installing clay and concrete tile over solid sheathing, cover the plywood with 15- or 30-lb. felt paper and install strapping over the plywood, cutting notches or shimming under battens for drainage. For optimum drainage and ventilation, install counterbattens.

Manufacturers make a ridge/hip tile with a 120° spread, as well as a 90° rake tile to match most concrete tile types. Some (but not all) also offer apex tiles for hip and ridge intersections and hip starter courses.

Concrete Tile Color

Tile color can either be integral or applied to the surface as an acrylic spray or slurry. Integral tiles are known as color-through. They come in fewer colors, and the colors are darker.

Freeze-Thaw Protection

Due to the impermeability of extruded concrete, freeze-thaw protection is generally much better with concrete tiles than with clay tiles.

Figure 34. Fastening Tile in High-Wind Areas

		Field Tile			Perimeter Tile and Tile Cantilevered Area[2]
	Roof Slope	Solid Sheathing with Battens	Solid Sheathing without Battens[1]	Eaves Course	
Fastening required on roofs 40 feet or less above ground (measured to the eaves) in areas with wind velocities up to 80 miles per hour	3:12 to 5:12	one 10d nail every tile	one 10d nail every tile	one 10d nail & one clip every tile[3]	one 10d nail every tile
	5:12 to less than 7:12	one 10d nail every tile	one 10d nail every tile	one 10d nail & one clip every tile[3]	one 10d nail every tile
	7:12 to less than 12:12	one 10d nail every tile	N/A	one 10d nail & one clip every tile[3]	one 10d nail every tile
	12:12 and over	one 10d nail and clip every tile	N/A	one 10d nail & one clip every tile[3]	one 10d nail and clip every tile
Fastening required on roofs 40 feet or less above ground (measured to the eaves) in areas with wind velocities up to 80 miles per hour	All slopes	one 12d nail or two 10d nails and one clip every tile		one 12d nail or two 10d nails and one clip every tile	one 12d nail or two 10d nails and one clip every tile
Fastening between 80 and 120 m.p.h.	All slopes	two 10d nails and one clip every tile		two 10d nails and one clip every tile	two 10d nails and one clip every tile

(1) For slopes exceeding 7:12, battens are required.

(2) Perimeter nailing areas include the distance equal to three tiles (but not less than 36") from the edges of hips, ridges, eaves, rakes, and major roof penetrations.

(3) You can use two nails per tile instead of clips.

For high-wind areas and tall buildings, the UBC currently requires one nail in the head of every tile, plus one nose clip for eaves tile and an extra nail for rake tiles. The National Tile Roofing Manufacturers Association recommends two nails or a nail and a clip for every tile in seismic and high-wind areas, and three fasteners for perimeter tiles. Check with your local officials for new code developments if you work in high-wind or seismic zones.

Figure 35. Twisted-Wire Fastening Method

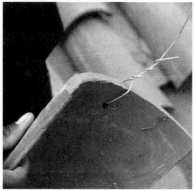

The twisted wire method uses a double strand of 14-gauge wire fastened at the ridge and eaves with special anchors (left). Each tile is secured with an individual tie-wire (center) that is threaded through the open loops in the twisted wire (right).

Sheathing and Underlayment

Sheathing Options for Tile

A tile roof can be installed either over a solid sheathing or spaced sheathing.

Underlayment Options for Tile

- For slopes 4:12 and over, solid sheathing and 30-lb. felt will do. See **Figure 32**, page 34.

- On solid sheathing, 1x2 battens are mounted to the roof deck over the underlayment and between the roof eaves and the ridge. Battens are required on roofs with slopes in excess of 7:12, and are generally recommended on all tile installations.

See **Figure 33,** page 35, for underlayment application over solid sheathing.

- Check manufacturers' suggested layout procedures. Each manufacturer should supply information regarding batten spacing and kick-strip installation, as well as a layout calculation chart for its product.

- Tiles on shallow slopes must be installed over a waterproof low-slope roof, either built-up or single-ply (see "Low-Slope and Flat Roofs," **pages 62** to **71**). In this case, the tiles are mostly decorative, although they do shield the membrane against ultraviolet light, high winds, and mechanical damage.

Figure 36. Fasteners for High-Wind Areas

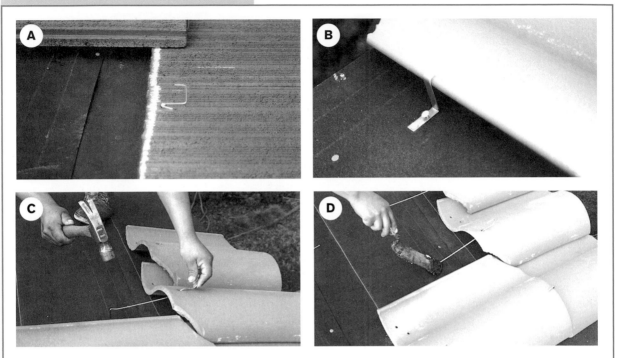

Nose clips (A and B) hold down the front end of the tile. The same nail secures both the nose clip and the tile underneath. **The Tile Nail®** from Newport Fasteners has several advantages over a conventional nose clip (C). Because it is driven in a few inches away from the tile, there is less risk of cracking the tile while nailing. Its length allows enough movement to keep the tile from breaking during high winds or an earthquake. Also, the holes can be patched with mastic to prevent leaks in the membrane (D).

- Flat concrete tiles should be installed over preservative-treated battens (**Figure 41**, page 43). In climates with snow accumulation, install the counter battens over battens that run from ridge to eaves (**Figure 33**). These enhance drainage and ventilation, and help to keep the roof uniformly cold, which lessens the chance of ice damming.

Anchoring Systems

Before installing tile, determine the type of anchoring system appropriate to prevailing conditions.

Mortar-Set

In areas where wind velocities approach 80 mph, tile is often set in a mortar bed over a built-up membrane.

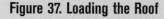

Figure 37. Loading the Roof

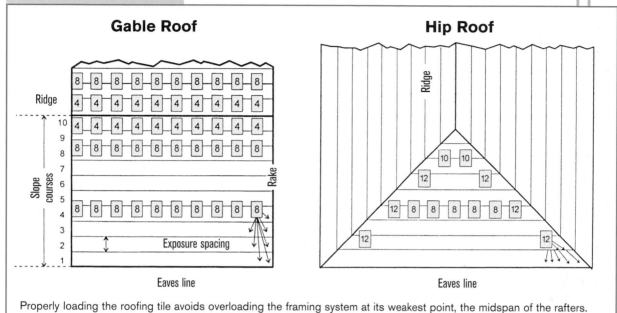

Properly loading the roofing tile avoids overloading the framing system at its weakest point, the midspan of the rafters.

Soak the tile before installation to reduce the chance of dry tile drawing moisture out of the mortar, and weakening the bond.

Nail-On

With the "nail-on" method, each roof tile is nailed directly to the roof sheathing (for low-slope roofs) or to a wooden batten attached to the sheathing. Nailing down the tiles is much faster and less labor-intensive than cementing tiles. Also, unlike the mud-on system, nailed tiles will "give" a little in big winds.

Nails for attaching tile. See **Figure 34**, page 36 for tips on fastening roof tile.

- Do not use smooth-shank nails; they will work their way out in heavy winds.

- Use either a ring-shank nail or a hot-dipped galvanized nail.

- Two nails are better than one for fastening roofing tile.

Twisted Wire Systems

Designed for 2:12 to 24:12 slope roofs, this system uses fewer nails, so it

Figure 38. Clay Tile Installation

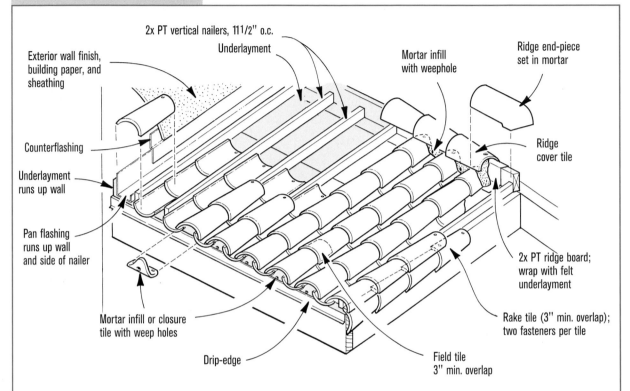

2x PT vertical nailers, 11 1/2" o.c.

Underlayment

Exterior wall finish, building paper, and sheathing

Mortar infill with weephole

Ridge end-piece set in mortar

Counterflashing

Ridge cover tile

Underlayment runs up wall

Pan flashing runs up wall and side of nailer

2x PT ridge board; wrap with felt underlayment

Mortar infill or closure tile with weep holes

Rake tile (3" min. overlap); two fasteners per tile

Drip-edge

Field tile 3" min. overlap

Typical installation of pan and cover clay tile: Vertical nailers are optional but can provide good support and anchoring for the cover tile. In some parts of the country, tile is wire tied, straw nailed, or attached with other types of fasteners.

punctures the waterproof underlayment less. Twisted wire systems are typically specified in earthquake zones and areas with moderate winds. Because the roof is not rigidly attached, the wire yields without transferring the shifting load caused by wind or seismic activity to the building.

- **Vertical wire runs.** The twisted wire system consists of two wires (12-gauge galvanized, with stainless or copper also available) wound together with an expanded loop or eyelet approximately every 6 in. The wires run from ridge to eaves between vertical courses of tile and are attached with approved anchors (**Figure 35**, page 37).

- **Anchor wires every 10 feet.** Nail or screw the twisted wires into the roof at the ridge, eaves, and every 10 ft. along the roof slope.

Figure 39. Concrete Tile Installation

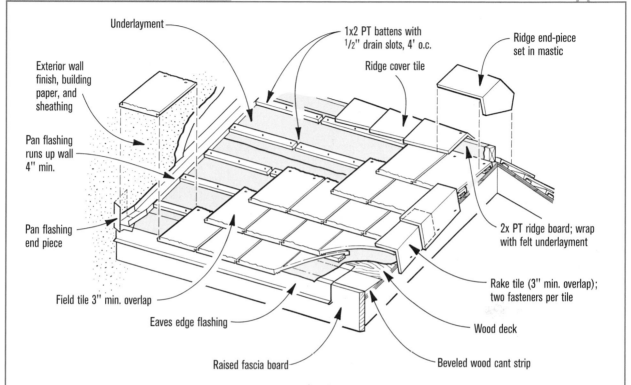

Underlayment

1x2 PT battens with
1/2" drain slots, 4' o.c.

Ridge cover tile

Ridge end-piece
set in mastic

Exterior wall
finish, building
paper, and
sheathing

Pan flashing
runs up wall
4" min.

Pan flashing
end piece

2x PT ridge board; wrap
with felt underlayment

Rake tile (3" min. overlap);
two fasteners per tile

Field tile 3" min. overlap

Eaves edge flashing

Wood deck

Raised fascia board

Beveled wood cant strip

Typical installation of flat-interlocking concrete tile: At the roof-to-wall connection, the underlayment is run up the wall 4 in. behind the pan flashing. The exterior wall finish acts as counterflashing and is held off the finish roofing. The pan flashing end-piece diverts water that runs down the pan flashing away from the wall finish.

- **Tie-wires secure tiles.** Secure individual tiles to the twisted wire with separate tie-wires. The individual tie-wires are threaded through the loops on the wire runs, then twisted closed.

- **Replacing damaged tile.** Damaged tiles fastened with the tie-wire system are easy to replace by folding back the damaged tile, untwisting the wires, and adding the new tile.

Fasteners for High-Wind Regions

Nose clips. Nail-on and twisted wire systems attach the tile only at the top — the butt end, or "nose," of the tile is free to rotate and break in a big wind. Special wire clips, known variously as nose clips, butt hooks, S hooks, and tile locks, provide a hold-down for the exposed edge of each cover tile (**Figure 36**, page 38).

Figure 40. Flashing Roof Penetrations

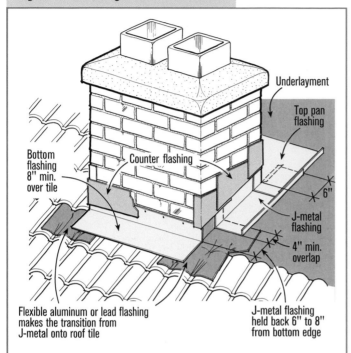

Underlayment

Top pan flashing

Bottom flashing 8" min. over tile

Counter flashing

6"

J-metal flashing

4" min. overlap

Flexible aluminum or lead flashing makes the transition from J-metal onto roof tile

J-metal flashing held back 6" to 8" from bottom edge

On a tile roof, the sides of dormers, skylights, and chimneys are flashed with galvanized pan flashing, which terminates on a piece of flexible aluminum. The aluminum flashing conducts water onto the top of tiles below the roof penetration.

Tile Nail. A new clip that functions as both a nail and a nose clip is the Tile Nail® (Newport Fasteners, Anaheim, Calif.). This is a 12-gauge galvanized wire (also available in brass or stainless) approximately 10 in. long with a $1\frac{1}{4}$-in. tail and a hook on the other end (**Figure 36**, page 38).

- Slip the end of the Tile Nail® through the hole in the tile, then nail it into the sheathing 6 in. above the tile — far enough away so there is no fear of breaking the tile.

- The next piece slips into the "nose" hook, positively restraining it as well as setting the head lap distance for the next course.

- "Butter" the nail end with roofing cement.

Hurricane clips. A less effective clip is a hurricane clip, or side strap made of 18-gauge galvanized steel. This is a locking device for the side edge of concrete, clay, and clay S tiles.

- Bend the clip into an L shape with the top curved to fit snugly over the side edge of the tile.

- Keep the bottom of the clip flat; nail or screw it to the sheathing or batten.

- Use nose clips to secure the front of tiles to keep them from "chattering," or worse, from prying the nail out or snapping the tile at the attachment point.

- Nose clips can be used with any combination of fasteners and are available in stainless, brass, and galvanized.

Figure 41. Eaves Details for Roofing Tile

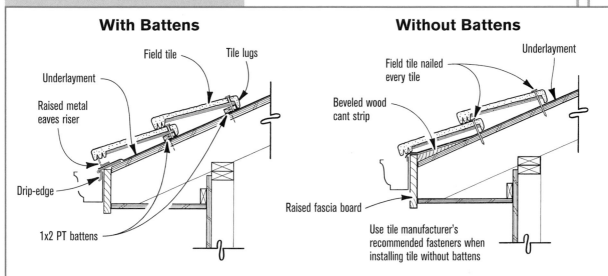

With Battens

Underlayment

Field tile

Tile lugs

Raised metal
eaves riser

Drip-edge

1x2 PT battens

Without Battens

Underlayment

Field tile nailed
every tile

Beveled wood
cant strip

Raised fascia board

Use tile manufacturer's
recommended fasteners when
installing tile without battens

Tile installed with battens and on raised metal eaves riser (left): Underlayment should overhang drip-edge and be completely weathertight. **Tile installed without battens** (right): Check with the tile manufacturer for proper nail type and nailing depth. A continuous cant strip stops water from collecting along raised fascia board. Underlayment should overhang drip-edge and be completely weathertight.

- Hurricane clips should be used only as a backup fastener to help roofs survive high winds. It's hard to get these clips to fit snugly to the tile, so after several storms they tend to bend and work loose.

Loading the Roof with Tile

Gable Roofs

On a gable roof, stack the tile to properly distribute the weight of the tile during installation. This avoids over-loading the roof framing system at its weakest point, the midspan of the rafters.

- Pick tiles from different pallets to avoid color patterning.

- Starting from the right, lay out the stacks in numbers as shown at left in **Figure 37**, page 39, beginning with the fourth course. Space stacks about 12 in. apart.

- Repeat the procedure every fourth course. Odd numbers of courses should have two additional tiles for each additional course on each stack along the ridge.

Hip Roofs

Loading a hip roof is the same as loading a gable roof except that the number of tiles in stacks at the far left may vary due to the size of the roof (**Figure 37**, page 39).

Cutting Tile

Straight cuts at rakes can be made by scoring a line on the tile, then breaking it with a roofing hatchet. Although this leaves a rough edge, it will be covered by the rake tiles.

Valley and hip cuts. Use a power saw — a cut-off saw or a standard tile saw — and a diamond blade. Tiles may be cut wet or dry. When dry cutting, workers should wear respirators because of the fine dust. Also sweep any accumulated dust off the roof so that it does not stain the tiles or cause a fall.

Installation Details for Tile

Most tile companies publish thorough installation manuals, so it's worthwhile to compare these before deciding on a particular brand.

Basic installation details for roofing tile are shown in **Figures 38** and **39**, pages 40-41.

Cold-climate eaves details. In cold climates with snow accumulation, install counterbattens over battens that run from eaves to ridge (**Figure 33**, page 35). These enhance drainage and ventilation, and help keep the roof uniformly cold to reduce the chance of ice damming.

Sidewall flashing requires a pan, as shown in **Figures 38** and **39**, pages 40-41.

Penetration flashing. The downhill corners of dormers, chimneys, and skylights should be flashed with both a flexible aluminum flashing, as well as a galvanized-steel pan flashing, as shown in **Figure 40**, page 42.

Clay and Concrete Tile

Tile Maintenance and Repairs

In general, problems with tile roofs are similar to those with slate roofs, and the maintenance procedures are the same (see "Slate," page 26).

Low-Slope Tile Repairs

On low slopes, a leaky, water-damaged subroof may be hidden by undamaged tiles. Unfortunately, the only way to fix a damaged subroof may be to tear off the tiles.

Working on Existing Tile

The most difficult part of repairing a few broken tiles is removing them without breaking the surrounding tiles. You can walk on flat shingle tiles if you're careful, but with high-profile tiles, lay down sheets of plywood, wide planks, or burlap bags filled with sand to spread your weight. In some cases, you can work off a ladder hooked to the ridge.

Removing Damaged Tile

Use a a slate ripper or hacksaw blade to cut the nails.

Attaching Replacement Tiles

Attach replacement tile with a copper nail, slate hook, or copper strap, as with slates (**Figure 27**, page 27).

Tile Reroofing

Always strip the old roofing material before applying a new clay or concrete tile roof. Most roof structures can't support the extra weight. If the old roofing is something other than slate or tile, then it may be necessary to reinforce the rafters.

Metal Panels

Traditional metal roofs are made from flat-lock metal and site-formed standing seam panels. However, the increasing majority of metal roofs are made from several types of pre-fab panels, including screw-down, ribbed panels (similar to those used on agricultural buildings), and "modular" metal panels that mimic shingle, shake, and tile roofing.

Flat-Lock Metal Roofs

What used to be called a "tin roof" is actually made from terne-coated steel. These days, it is used mostly on restoration projects. These roofs have a series of rectangular metal panels, or pans, folded together along the edges. The seams must be beaten flat with a mallet, and then hand-soldered.

Slope

Flat-lock roofing is called for on any roof with a pitch less than 3:12. On steeper roofs, standing-seam metal should be used.

Flat-Lock Metals

Terneplate. This is the most common and inexpensive material used for flat-lock metal roofs. Originally, terne metal was a copper-bearing steel coated

Figure 42. Flat-Lock Panel Pattern

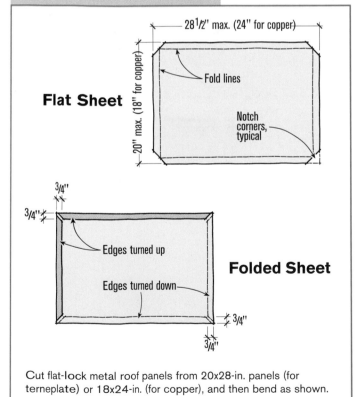

Flat Sheet

28 1/2" max. (24" for copper)

20" max. (18" for copper)

Fold lines

Notch corners, typical

3/4"

3/4"

Edges turned up

Folded Sheet

Edges turned down

3/4"

3/4"

Cut flat-lock metal roof panels from 20x28-in. panels (for terneplate) or 18x24-in. (for copper), and then bend as shown.

on both sides with an alloy of 80% lead and 20% tin. Since lead was outlawed, only Terne II coated steel, using a 50% zinc, 50% tin alloy coating, is available (Follansbee Steel, 800/624-6906, www.follansbeeroofing.com). This material comes in precut 20x28-in. panels or 28-in.-wide coil stock.

Unfinished terneplate must be painted on the underside before installation, and on the top side after installation. Use a rapid-dry water-based acrylic from Follansbee that is formulated specifically for Terne II. Typically, roofs should be repainted every 10 or 12 years.

Prefinished terneplate cannot be soldered; it is used for field-formed standing seam, not for flat-lock roofs.

TCS (terne-coated stainless steel) is a traditional material that doesn't need to be painted to prevent the base metal from corroding. However, it has the same silver color as unfinished terneplate and may be painted for appearance.

Copper is expensive but looks great. Be forewarned that the runoff stains the house. Copper also expands and contracts more than steel, so it should be used only on short roof runs.

Figure 43. Flat-Lock Panel Layout

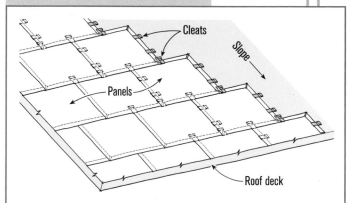

A typical layout shows how the staggered pans cover the roof. Uphill pans should always overlap the edges of lower pans.

Lead-coated copper used to be a popular choice but is no longer widely available; existing roofs are often painted for appearance with a slow-drying linseed-oil-based paint.

Flat-Lock Installation Checklist

- Prepaint the underside of Terne II panels, including all cleats, flashing, and drip-edge stock using a rapid-dry acrylic paint. Never use an aluminized paint, which will promote galvanic corrosion (see "Galvanic Corrosion," page 77).

- Lay roofing panels over a wood deck, preferably plywood. Do not use treated wood; the salts will attack the metal coating.

- Install metal panels over a rosin-paper slip sheet. Do not use asphalt-impregnated felt; the asphalt will attack the metal coating.

- Form pans from 20x28-in. sheets, using a metal brake (see pattern, **Figure 42**, page 46).

- Panel edges along rakes and eaves lock over a drip-edge flashing (follow standing-seam detail, **Figure 47**, page 52). Lock panels to L-flashing bent from Terne II metal at vertical walls.

- Stagger panels, and secure to roof deck, as shown in **Figure 43**, page 47.

- Use 2x4-in. prepainted cleats and two 1-in.-long roofing nails to secure panels. Fold over flap on cleat to cover fastener heads.

- Fold seams closed, crimp tightly, and beat down with a mallet and wood block. Seams should be single locked a minimum of $1/2$ inch.

- Solder seams with a 50/50 solder and rosin flux, using a 3-pound minimum soldering iron. Be sure to wipe off all excess flux.

- Paint soldered roof with a minimum two coats of the same rapid-dry acrylic paint used to prepaint the underside of the panels.

Traditional Standing Seam

Standing-seam roofs shed snow accumulations quickly. Standing seam is a good choice for steep gable and shed roofs in cold climates.

Ordering Standing-Seam Metal

Traditional standing-seam roofs can be field-formed using the same materials used for flat-lock metal roofs. Pans are attached to the roof deck with cleats along one edge, while the seam along the other edge is covered by the next pan (**Figure 44**).

Preformed pans made of terneplate (24- or 20-in. wide) are available from Follansbee Steel (800/624-6906, www.follansbeeroofing.com).

Panel length. Standard lengths for preformed pan are 8-, 10-, and 12-ft. It's hard to handle a pan longer than 8 ft. without wrinkling the metal.

- When figuring pan lengths, allow extra for cross-seams and ridge seams (**Figure 45**).

- For shallow roofs (less than 6:12), allow a minimum 4-in. overlap, plus an additional couple of inches to form a deeper cross seam that accommodates a cross-seam connector strip (**Figure 45**).

- Do not use standing-seam panels below 3:12.

Number of pans. Measure the roof and plan for a standing seam at the centerline. Make a sketch showing the layout of the pans on the roof, and then calculate the number of pans you'll need (**Figure 46**).

Width of gable-end pans. At gable ends, cut off the upstand on the gable side of a preformed pan, and allow a $1/2$-in. fold over a drip-edge. This will reduce the pan width on the roof by $1^1/2$ in. (**Figure 47**, page 52).

Standing-Seam Installation Checklist

- Roll out rosin paper as a slip-sheet between the roof deck and the pans. Do not use roofing felt, as the asphalt will attack the metal.

- Snap chalklines at the position of each vertical seam to help keep seams straight.

- Start at the bottom left edge of the roof and hook the first pan into the drip-edges.

- Using a mallet and a block of hardwood, flatten the seams at the drip-edges. Then, using locking-plier

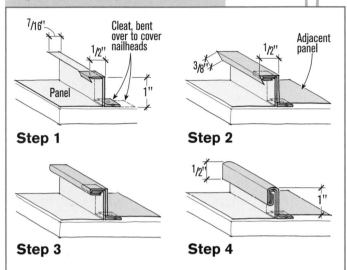

Figure 44. Standing-Seam Detail

Step 1
Step 2
Step 3
Step 4

To secure a standing seam panel, a metal cleat (1) is bent over the panel stand (2), then nailed to the roof deck. The adjacent panel fits over the two pieces (3) and the entire seam is folded closed (4).

crimpers or roofing tongs, crimp the pan/drip-edge seam tightly together.

- Install hold-down cleats at 12-in. spacing up the right side of the pan and across the top edge of the pan. Fasten the cleats to the deck with two 1-in. roofing nails. Use prepainted terne or TCS cleats fastened with galvanized nails. For copper pans, use copper cleats and copper nails. Fold the tail of the cleats over the nail heads.

Figure 45. Standing-Seam Panel Joints

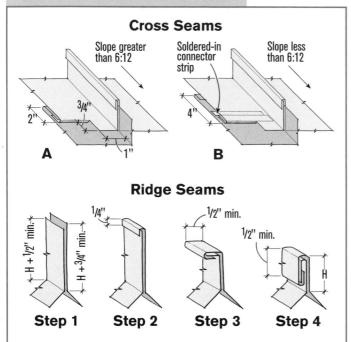

Cross Seams

Slope greater than 6:12

Soldered-in connector strip

Slope less than 6:12

3/4"

2"

1"

A

4"

B

Ridge Seams

1/4"

H + 1/2" min.

H + 3/4" min.

1/2" min.

1/2" min.

H

Step 1   **Step 2**   **Step 3**   **Step 4**

Cross seams: Use a standard cross seam (A) on roofs greater than 6:12. Roofs less than 6:12 require a more watertight cross seam (B), using a soldered-in cleat. **Ridge seams:** The stand at the ridge should be a minimum of 1 in. (H).

- Install the second pan above the first by hooking it into the top of the first pan and into the drip-edge. Close the seam at the drip-edge as before. Flatten the cross-seam between the two pans with a mallet and wood block.

- Anchor the second pan with cleats, and then install the remainder of

the first row of pans all the way to the ridge of the roof.

- Install the first pan of the next row by hooking the triple bend over the double bend and sliding the pan up until it hooks on the drip-edge. Crimp the seam at the drip-edge, and install cleats along the right edge and top edge of the pan.

- Fold the first standing seam closed, as shown in **Figure 48**.

- Install the rest of the pans. Remember to stagger the cross-seams and keep the pans aligned with your chalklines.

Modern standing-seam panels are factory-formed from prefinished galvanized or Galvalume-coated steel (see "Metal Panel Coatings," page 54). These panels are made to custom dimensions and factory-formed with seams that snap in place. Some panel systems use cleats (or "clips"), but more commonly on residential products, the panels have a screw-flange along one edge of the panel that is concealed by the next panel.

Modern standing-seam panels are treated here as one variation of a prefab, vertical seam panel. A standing-seam profile will not leave voids in valleys like a ribbed panel; it is a good choice for complex roofs that must be made watertight (**Figure 44**, page 49).

Pre-Fab Metal Panels

Similar to "ag panels" that have kept barns dry for years, pre-fab, vertical-seam panels typically use exposed fasteners — usually a screw with a rubber gasket. Some (particularly those with a standing-seam profile) use concealed clips or screws. Pre-fab panels are typically less expensive than field-formed standing-seam and are considerably easier for contractors to install without specialized equipment.

Steel. Most metal roofing panels are made of steel. All steel panels have a metallic coating, and may also have a paint finish. The most common thicknesses of steel roofing panels are 24-, 26-, and 29-gauge. (The higher the number, the thinner the metal.)

Aluminum. Some vertical-seam roofing panels are made with an aluminum base metal. Not to be confused with an aluminized coating (see "Metal Panel Coatings," page 54), aluminum panels

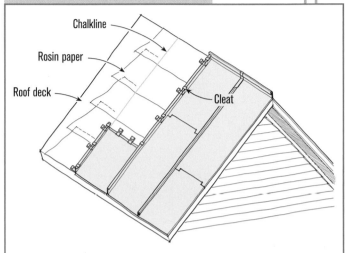

Figure 46. Standing-Seam Layout

Chalkline
Rosin paper
Roof deck
Cleat

Installing a standing-seam roof is a lot like hanging wallpaper: Small errors at the beginning of the run create impossible problems at the end. Snap chalklines over a rosin-paper slip sheet to guide the installation.

are much more corrosion-resistant than steel panels. Residential "modular" panels may be as thin as .015 to .02 in. For larger vertical-seam panels, opt for a commercial-grade aluminum at .032-in.-thick.

Aluminum also has an increased potential for expansion and contraction with changes in temperature (see "Thermal Response of Metal," page 52). This is not a problem for a small modular panel, but long vertical-seam aluminum panels should be installed panels over Z-channel purlins with clips, per manufacturer's instructions (**Figure 49**, page 54).

Figure 47. Standing-Seam Edge Detail

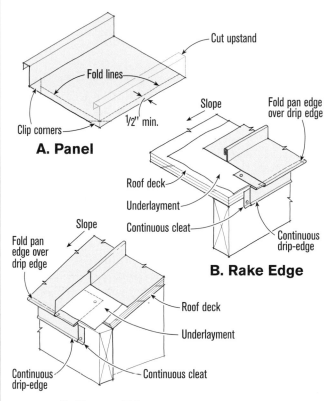

A. Panel

Cut upstand

Fold lines

Clip corners

1/2" min.

B. Rake Edge

Slope

Fold pan edge over drip edge

Roof deck

Underlayment

Continuous cleat

Continuous drip-edge

C. Eaves Edge

Slope

Fold pan edge over drip edge

Roof deck

Underlayment

Continuous drip-edge

Continuous cleat

On a corner panel (along a gable end), cut off the upstand, then clip the pan corner at 45 degrees, as shown (A). Install a continuous drip-edge around the roof perimeter, then fold the edges of the pan 3/4 in. over this drip-edge, and lock in place with crimpers.

Rib profiles. The rib pattern in vertical-seam metal roofing varies from manufacturer to manufacturer and region to region. In the Northeast and Southeast, a popular profile is called "5-V crimp," which has a 24-in.-wide exposure, with a double-vee profile along each edge and a single-vee profile down the center.

For cold, wet climates where ice dams and snow accumulations may occur, use a panel with the narrowest possible rib. The narrower the rib, the easier it is to seal.

Thermal Response of Metal

Metal expands and contracts with changes in temperature, which can be quite extreme on a roof. For example, in winter, it's not unusual for a roof panel to go from 180°F on a sunny day to below 0° at night. Under these conditions, a 20-ft.-long steel panel would expand over 1/4 in. An aluminum panel this size would expand more than 1/2 in. If attached to plywood sheathing, the panel will "crown" between fasteners, and the force can cause screws to shear or the metal to tear around screws.

Evaluate the expected amount of change (**Figure 50**). If the change in the length of the panel exceeds .15 in., consider these strategies:

- Reduce panel length;

- Install panels over Z-channel to absorb movement (**Figure 49**);

- Choose a light (preferably white) panel in hot climates to reduce panel temperature.

Galvanic Corrosion

Do not combine dissimilar metals. Always use fasteners, clips, purlins, and flashings of a similar or compatible metal. For a complete understanding of this, see description under "Flashing: Galvanic Corrosion," page 77.

- Don't use a pencil to mark cuts and fastener layouts. Graphite is listed on the galvanic scale and can corrode a roofing panel's metallic coating. Use a felt-tipped marker.

Fasteners for Metal Roofs

Pre-fab metal roof panels may have exposed or concealed fasteners.

Exposed fasteners for metal roofs are usually screws with rubber washers.

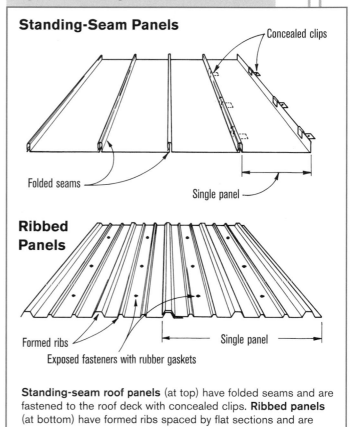

Figure 48. Standing-Seam vs. Ribbed Panels

Standing-Seam Panels

Concealed clips

Folded seams

Single panel

Ribbed Panels

Formed ribs

Exposed fasteners with rubber gaskets

Single panel

Standing-seam roof panels (at top) have folded seams and are fastened to the roof deck with concealed clips. **Ribbed panels** (at bottom) have formed ribs spaced by flat sections and are secured with exposed fasteners.

Always install the screw in the flat portion of the panel, not on the raised rib. The rubber washer will seal around the screw. If installed through the rib, the screw will not get enough purchase to hold the panel securely, and because most of its length is unsupported, it may shear easily. Both increase the chances for blow-off.

Figure 49. Thermal Response Over Z-Channel

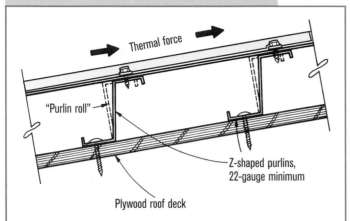

Thermal force

"Purlin roll"

Z-shaped purlins, 22-gauge minimum

Plywood roof deck

Metal roof panels installed over Z-shaped purlins will "roll" with thermal expansion of the panels. Wood strapping or hat channel will not absorb thermal expansion as well.

Concealed fasteners for metal roofing may be a screw inserted through a concealed flange or through a panel clip designed to absorb expansion.

- Never use nails. The increased expansion and contraction of the panels will eventually work nails loose.

- Use screws that penetrate all the way through the sheathing $1/4$- to $1/2$-in.

Ordering Metal Roof Panels

Agricultural panels may be sold in standard lengths, but most residential roofing panels are often ordered in any length (down to the fraction of an inch) from a lumberyard or roofing supplier. In general, the length of the panels will be the ridge-to-eaves measurement.

- In most cases, the $1^1/2$ in. added for the eaves overhang is balanced by the $1^1/2$ in. subtracted for ventilation at the ridge.

- The cap flashing installed at the ridge will allow room to fudge 1 or 2 in. at the top.

Metal Panel Coatings

All sheet steel is coated with a thin layer of corrosion-resistant metal.

Galvanized

The most common coating is pure zinc, known as a galvanized coating, which oxidizes, chemically sealing the base metal from corrosion.

- The thickness of a galvanized coating is designated as G-60, G-90, or G-100. The number here refers to minimum application rates equal to .60, .90, and 1.0 ounce of zinc per sq. ft. (total coating thickness both sides).

- Zinc is water soluble. As it dissolves, it tends to recoat scratches or cut ends and is considered "self-healing." However, because the coating dissolves, it eventually washes away and the base metal begins to rust. The thicker the coating, the longer the panel will last.

Aluminized

Pure aluminum coatings over steel carry a Type II designation. (Type I is used in the automotive industry.) Owing to the truly inert nature of aluminum, these coatings don't dissolve or wear away, providing significantly better protection than galvanizing.

Galvalume

Also known as *Zincalume* (if the panel manufacturer originated in Australia or New Zealand) this coating is made from an aluminum-zinc alloy. The typical coating weight AZ-55 designates 55% aluminum and 45% zinc by weight. As one might expect, Galvalume falls between a pure zinc and a pure aluminum coating in its performance.

Figure 50. Calculating Thermal Response of Metal

To get an accurate measurement of how much a metal panel will move in any climate, use the formula:

$$\Delta L = \Delta T \times L \times Ce$$

ΔL = the change in length of the panel
ΔT = the change in surface temperature throughout the year (in °F)
L = the panel length (in inches)
Ce = the coefficient of expansion for the panel material (see list below)

Coefficients of Expansion for Metal Roofs

Steel	.0000067
Copper	.0000094
Aluminum	.0000129
Stainless	.0000096

Paints for Metal Roofing

Nearly all roofing panels have some type of factory-applied finish over the metallic coating.

Finish Warranty

Factory-applied paint rarely peels, but eventually will fade. It usually fades unevenly, so it looks unsightly. When a paint fades, it's a breakdown of the pigment. Depending on the quality of the paint resin, which creates a protective coating around the pigment, panel

Figure 51. Wall Flashing for Metal Roofs

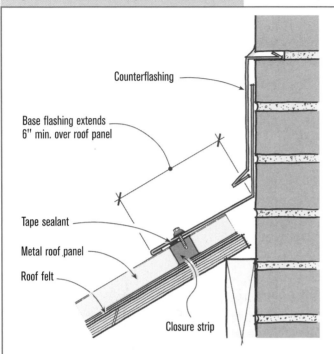

Counterflashing

Base flashing extends
6" min. over roof panel

Tape sealant

Metal roof panel

Roof felt

Closure strip

Use a two-piece metal flashing to accommodate the differential movement between walls (or chimneys, skylights, and roof hatches) and metal roof panels. Fasten the base flashing to the roof panel, but not to the counterflashing.

manufacturers will warrant the finish against fading. However, the warranty period on the finish is considerably shorter than the warranty against corrosion of the base metal.

Color Choices

Red, bright blue, and black pigments tend to fade the fastest. Grey (the lighter the better), tan, and white fade the least.

Paint Resins

Better quality resins in paints bond tighter and provide better protection, but even the best ones eventually chalk. There are three types:

- **Polyester resins** are the least expensive and of the lowest quality.

- **Silicon-modified resins** will retain their gloss much longer than polyesters.

- **Fluoropolymers**, known by such brand names as Kynar® and Fluropon®, are the most expensive and longest lasting. The more resin, the longer the finish lasts. Top-quality panels typically use a 70% formulation, while less expensive products advertising this superior resin use thinner concentrations.

Field-applied paints

These will last only 5 to 7 years before peeling, even if applied under the best conditions.

Metal-Panel Sealing Details

House roofs with dormers, hips, valleys, chimneys, skylights, and plumbing vent penetrations put more demands on metal roofs. Metal roofs on houses must be built watertight by sealing all joints, side seams, and endlaps.

Sealants for Metal Panels

Thermal movement, freeze-thaw cycles, and exposure to ultraviolet light will degrade even the best quality sealants. For best results:

- Use butyl tape ($1/2$-in.-wide works well for panel seams). Tape sealants, which have a high solids content (about 97%), don't shrink as much as gun-grade sealants. Most tapes for metal panels are butyl polymers, which will last 30 years or more if protected from exposure to ultraviolet light. Gun-grade sealants are usually about 70% solids, which means that when the 30% solvent evaporates, the sealant shrinks.

- Do not use silicone. Many silicone sealants contain acids, which can damage metallic coatings. Also, silicone has poor adhesive strength on metal. If butyl tape is not available, use a urethane instead.

- Always seal between panels, so the sealant is hidden from the damages of ultraviolet light. Sealants smeared on the exterior of the panel will surely fail.

- At eaves, in valleys, and on the upslope side of chimneys and skylights, use rubber closure strips to seal the void created by the profile of the panel ribs. Most panel suppliers offer these closure strips in both male and female (inside and out-

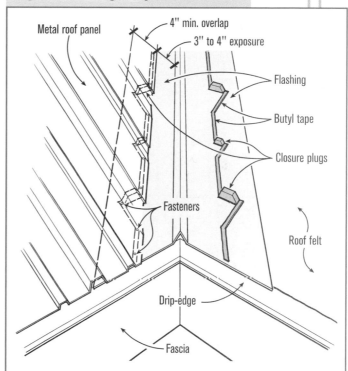

Figure 52. Sealing Valleys in Metal Roofs

Metal roof panel — 4" min. overlap — 3" to 4" exposure — Flashing — Butyl tape — Closure plugs — Fasteners — Roof felt — Drip-edge — Fascia

Seal the diagonal valley cuts on the roof panel with plugs cut from a closure strip. The plugs must be positioned square to the panel's length and sealed top and bottom with butyl tape.

side) configurations. Make sure a metal panel or flashing extends over the rubber closure to protect it from sunlight.

Wall Flashing For Metal Roofs

When flashing against walls — as well as skylights, chimneys, and roof hatches — use a two-piece flashing with closure strips (rubber blocks that mirror

Figure 53. Sealing Vertical Seams

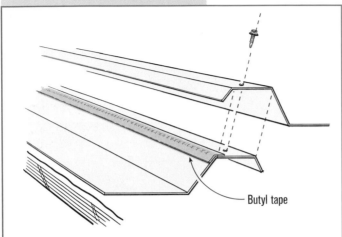

— Butyl tape

To seal the lap between adjacent panels, apply butyl tape to the weather side of the rib shoulder.

the panel profile) or preformed curb flashings (**Figure 51**).

- Connect the base flashing to the roof panel with washered screws.

- Apply tape sealant between the roof panel and the flash-ing, and be sure the screw pierces the sealant or is placed on the dry side of the tape, not on the weather side.

- Seal the joint between the base flashing and the roof panel with tape sealant.

- On the upslope side of a chimney or skylight, use a cricket, or diverter, to direct the flow of water around the penetration (see "Flashing

Chimneys," page 86). This cricket should be inserted beneath the upslope panel, sealed with butyl tape, and the voids at the cut edges of the roof panel sealed with rubber closure strips.

Sealing Valleys

Cutting a panel diagonally across a rib produces a large irregularly shaped void that is difficult to close.

- Use a valley flashing made from flat stock with the same coating and finish as the roof panels. Bend it to the roof slopes with an inverted "V" at the centerline (see "Open Valleys," page 80).

- Cut off the rib portion of a standard male closure so you are left with several "plugs." Position these plugs square to the panel's length.

- Install roof panels at least 3 to 4 in. upslope of the valley centerline, and make sure the flashing extends at least 4 in. past the panel edge so the closures seal to the flashing.

- When installing roof panels over the valley flashing, apply tape sealant on the top and bottom of the plugs, and use a close fastener spacing in the pattern shown in **Figure 52**. Screws must pierce the sealant or be placed on the dry side of the joint.

- On long valleys, use several valley sections to avoid problems with thermal expansion. Overlap the sections at least 3 in. and use a double row of tape sealant.

Sealing Round Penetrations

Round penetrations, such as plumbing vents and furnace flues, must be flashed with special rubber boot jacks that have a moldable aluminum compression ring (available from specialty contractor and commercial roof suppliers).

Sealing Vertical Seams

- Apply the tape to the top shoulder of the panel rib, making sure that the majority of the sealant winds up on the weather side of any fasteners (**Figure 53**).

- Do not peel away the release paper until you're ready to install the overlapping panel. Align the panel exactly before it contacts the sealant. Once a panel touches the tape, even a small adjustment is difficult.

- Screw panel sides together, piercing through the sealant on the "dry" side with $^3/_4$in.-long $^1/_4$ x14 hex head galvanized screws with a #1 drill point.

Figure 54. Sealing Panel Endlaps

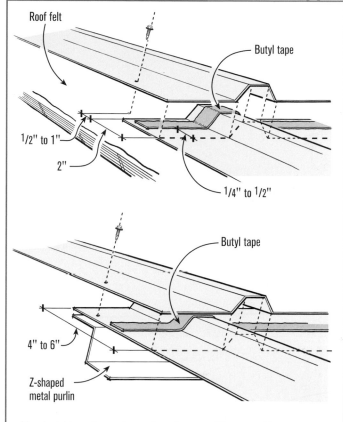

Roof felt

Butyl tape

$^1/_2$" to 1"

2"

$^1/_4$" to $^1/_2$"

Butyl tape

4" to 6"

Z-shaped metal purlin

Use butyl tape to seal panel endlaps, making sure the screws that fasten the panel to the deck (at top) or to purlins and sleepers (at bottom) are placed above the sealant, as shown.

Sealing Endlaps

- Make sure the upslope panel always overlaps the downslope panel (**Figure 54**).

- Apply sealant on the weather side of the endlap fasteners.

Figure 55. Sealing Eaves

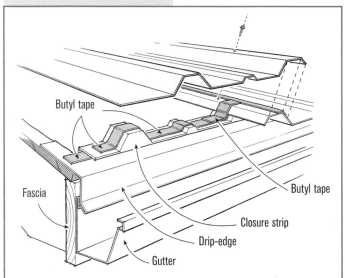

Butyl tape

Fascia

Butyl tape

Closure strip

Drip-edge

Gutter

When gutters are used, seal the eaves as if they will be submerged in water. Without gutters, roof panels should overhang the drip-edge at least 4 in.

• If gutters are used, take extra care to seal with rubber closures and butyl tape to prevent snow, rain, and ice from entering the panel voids (**Figure 55**).

Sealing Rakes

Prefabricated commercial rake flashings are available, but these are usually too large and "boxy" for use on a residence. Instead, ask the panel supplier to furnish flat sheet stock with a matching finish to be bent into a simple L-flashing, as shown in **Figure 56**.

• Attach L-flashing to the roof at a high rib with sealant tape. This might mean extending the horizontal leg a few extra inches.

• Fasten the L-flashing to the fascia using a metal cleat that matches the angle of the drip leg. (Alternatively, fasten through the face of the flashing with a washered screw.)

Hip and Ridge Caps

Most panel suppliers offer standard ridge components for use with their panels.

• Place screws that secure the panel to the deck (or purlins) above the end-lap sealant.

Sealing Eaves

• Drip flashing should be nailed down just enough to hold it in place prior to installing the roof panels.

• Screws to hold down roof panels should pierce through the panel, drip flashing, and deck.

- Use a sealant tape to seal the joint between roof panel and ridge cap.

- When using long panels that are subject to substantial thermal movement, make sure the ridge cap and the panels are fastened separately to the deck.

- For hips, metal roof manufacturers typically provide metal J-trim, which is topped by a metal ridge cap (**Figure 57**).

- On complex roofs where snowmelt and ice damming patterns are difficult to predict, make the hip assembly watertight with plug closures and tape sealant.

Reroofing with Metal

- If there are two or more layers of shingles, the roof should be stripped to the sheathing.

- If there is a single layer of shingles, and the shingles aren't curled, metal panels can be installed over wood strapping or purlins.

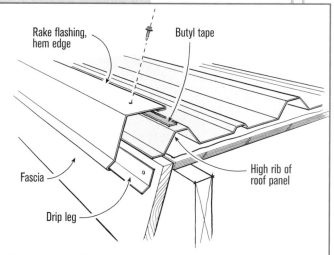

Figure 56. Rake Flashing

Rake flashing, hem edge

Butyl tape

Fascia

Drip leg

High rib of roof panel

Fabricate rake flashing from flat sheet stock provided by the roof panel manufacturer. Extend the horizontal leg of the flashing so it attaches with butyl tape and screws to the roof at a high rib.

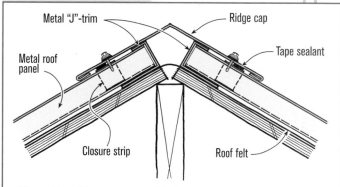

Figure 57. Sealing Hips

Metal "J"-trim

Ridge cap

Metal roof panel

Tape sealant

Closure strip

Roof felt

To seal hip ridges, use metal J-trim set square to the panel's length. On simple hips in steep roofs, this assembly can be installed without tape sealant; on complex or low-slope roofs, use with rubber closures and butyl tape.

Low-Slope and Flat Roofs

Low-slope roofs are those with slopes between 2:12 and 4:12. Flat roofs are those with slopes below 2:12. To prevent standing water, flat roofs should slope at least 1/4 in. per foot.

Roof Covering Choices

Roll roofing is a good, inexpensive choice for sheds or other outbuildings, but the best materials for residential flat and low-slope roofs are now the single-ply membranes. There are many single-ply membranes on the market, but the most proven are modified bitumen, EPDM rubber, and PVC. Some manufacturers sell only to certified installers and only for commercial installations. Refer to **Figure 58** for information regarding these different materials.

Roll Roofing

Roll roofing is similar in composition to asphalt shingles. It comes in 3-ft.-wide rolls that include an asphalt-impregnated organic or fiberglass mat and mineral granule surfacing.

Installing Roll Roofing

Roll roofing may be single- or double-coverage, as in **Figure 59**.

Single-coverage roofing has only a 2-in. overlap and exposed nails.

Double-coverage. This two-ply system uses about twice as much material as single coverage, but results in a more durable and watertight roof. In this case, the nails are hidden by the overlying course and sealed with lap cement.

Repairing Roll Roofing

Repair roll roofing by cutting away the damaged area and cementing in an oversized patch.

EPDM Rubber

EPDM (ethylene propylene diene monomer) is a single-ply, synthetic, rubber roofing membrane. It is dimensionally stable across a wide temperature range, so it puts less stress on flashings than other roof systems and retains its strength at extreme temperatures.

Figure 58. Roofing Materials For Low-Slope and Flat Roofs

Product	Advantages	Disadvantages
Roll Roofing	• Easy to install • Least expensive • Can have exposed nails on roofs with slopes 2:12 and above. Double coverage, with concealed nails, can be used on roofs with slopes of 1:12	• Short life expectancy (5 to 12 years depending on weather conditions) • Tendency to curl during installation • Should not use in temperatures below 45°F • Class "C" fire rating for both single & double coverage types
Built-Up Roofing	• Life expectancy 15 to 20 years (depending on the number of plies in the roof membrane and the method of application)	• Installed by specialists • Heavy equipment needed on site
Hot-Mopped Modified Bitumen	• Installation techniques based on BUR techniques • Slop in liquid bitumen can seal small holes	• Heavy equipment needed on site • Hot, dirty conditions during application may affect quality control
Self-Adhering Modified Bitumen	• Ease of installation • Minor adjustments of sheet placement are possible	• Needs careful substrate preparation; may be too much dust after tearoff to use self-adhering system • Rain-lapped application difficult on higher slopes
Torch-Applied Modified Bitumen	• Low-temperature applications (20°F) possible • Simple flashing of penetrations and terminations • Good adherence and good seams with experienced application	• Fire hazard from use of torches and flammable deck materials and cant strips • Client's and builder's insurance may not cover open-flame application • Worker's judgment required for proper flow of heated surface
EPDM	• Good resistance to ozone, UV light, weathering, and abrasion • Comes in larger sheets than PVC • Resistant to some acids, alkalis, ketones, esters and alcohols • Retains strength in extreme temperatures • Very stable across wide temperature range; less stress on flashings • Life expectancy 15 to 20 years	• Membrane swells and distorts with exposure to various solvents and animal/vegetable oils • Lap seams are weak • Usually comes in black only; available in white at greater cost • Less puncture-resistant than asphaltic products
PVC	• Stronger seams than EPDM; lap seams are "welded" • Available in white, grey, and other light colors	• Life expectancy averages $8^1/2$ years (less than EPDM) • Less resistant to chemicals than EPDM; inferior puncture resistance • Membrane prone to shattering with cold temperatures • Easily damaged by contact with asphalt

Figure 59. Roll Roofing Installation: Single- and Double-Coverage

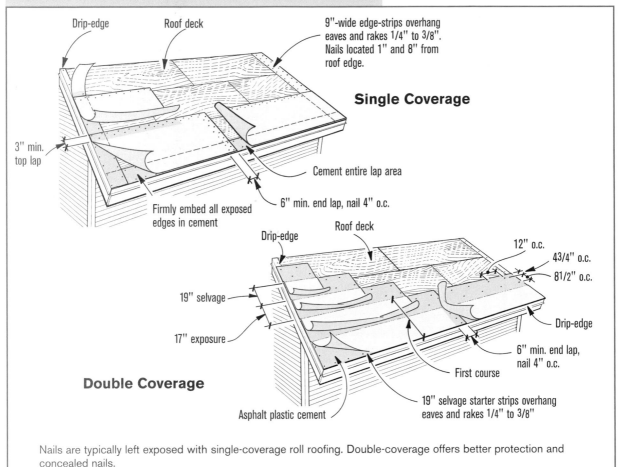

Drip-edge

Roof deck

9"-wide edge-strips overhang eaves and rakes 1/4" to 3/8". Nails located 1" and 8" from roof edge.

Single Coverage

3" min. top lap

Cement entire lap area

Firmly embed all exposed edges in cement

6" min. end lap, nail 4" o.c.

Drip-edge

Roof deck

12" o.c.

43/4" o.c.

81/2" o.c.

19" selvage

Drip-edge

17" exposure

6" min. end lap, nail 4" o.c.

Double Coverage

First course

Asphalt plastic cement

19" selvage starter strips overhang eaves and rakes 1/4" to 3/8"

Nails are typically left exposed with single-coverage roll roofing. Double-coverage offers better protection and concealed nails.

Because the sheets are big, ranging in size from 50x50 ft. to 50x200 ft., lap splices can be kept to a minimum (lap splices are a weak link in most roofing membranes).

Selecting EPDM Roofing

EPDM sheets can be fully adhered or mechanically attached with special fittings. On residential projects, fully-adhered systems prove to be the most practical.

Figure 60. EPDM Edge and Roof-to-Wall Details

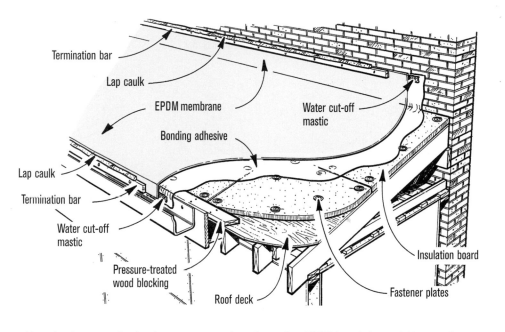

Termination bar

Lap caulk

EPDM membrane

Water cut-off mastic

Bonding adhesive

Lap caulk

Termination bar

Water cut-off mastic

Pressure-treated wood blocking

Roof deck

Insulation board

Fastener plates

Use aluminum termination bars to secure the edges of an EPDM roof. A special lap caulk protects the top of the termination bar, while a water-block tape or mastic seals the bottom edge of the membrane.

Availability

EPDM is available in two thicknesses: .045 in. and .060 in. The .060-in. or 60-mil EPDM lies flatter, wrinkles less, and is more durable than the 45-mil material.

EPDM membranes are usually black. If excessive heat buildup is a problem, however, they're also available in white (at a premium).

Durability

EPDM has excellent UV resistance, so it requires no further covering for protection from sunlight. It deteriorates about 1 mil per year, but its life span is usually guaranteed by the manufacturer in the 15- to 20-year range.

EPDM will stretch without tearing, and it holds up well to the rigors of installation. It also performs well in

Figure 61. Turning Corners with EPDM

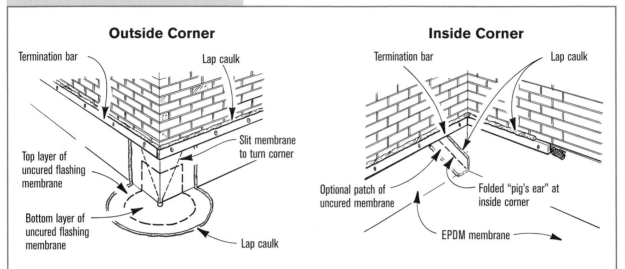

At outside corners, slit the membrane and apply a two-layer patch of uncured flashing membrane. Inside corners can be either slit and patched like an outside corner, or folded and secured with a termination bar.

extreme temperatures. Typical products will stay flexible down to 49°F and resist heat up to 300°F without cracking or deforming.

Avoid Grease and Solvents

EPDM should not be exposed to grease, solvents, oils, or petroleum products; fortunately, these are not usually a factor on residential roofs.

Decks over EPDM

EPDM can be covered with a wood deck on pressure-treated sleepers, with outdoor carpet or Astroturf, and even with concrete pavers.

Painting EPDM

EPDM can be painted with Hypalon paint, but the paint will have to be recoated every three or four years. (If you use EPDM on a rooftop deck, you should warn the homeowner about grease spills from a grill.)

Fully-Adhered EPDM

The most practical method for installing EPDM on a residential project is to install a fully-adhered system where the membrane is installed over foam board made with a special glass-fiber-reinforced felt skin that is compatible with EPDM adhesive.

Foam-Board Substrate

- Attach the foam board to the roof deck with screws and large metal plates installed on 2-ft. centers in both dimensions (**Figure 60**, page 65). The fasteners sit slightly proud of the surface, so the plates show through the rubber with the manufacturer's distinct dimple pattern. That way, for warranty work, the manufacturer's inspector can identify and count the plates.

Membrane

- Spread the rough-sized membrane sheet out on the deck, smooth out the wrinkles, and get it into final position. Then roll the sheet back onto itself halfway.

- Using rollers, spread the contact-type adhesive on both the rubber and deck.

- Once the adhesive is dry, carefully roll the membrane back into place and brush the surface with a stiff deck broom for good adhesion.

- Repeat the process for the other half of the sheet.

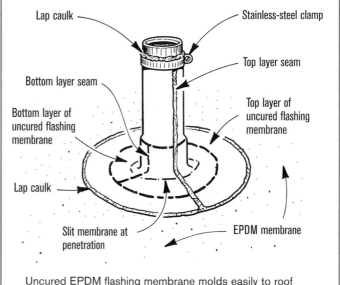

Figure 62. Sealing around a Vent Pipe with EPDM

Lap caulk — Stainless-steel clamp — Top layer seam — Bottom layer seam — Bottom layer of uncured flashing membrane — Top layer of uncured flashing membrane — Lap caulk — Slit membrane at penetration — EPDM membrane

Uncured EPDM flashing membrane molds easily to roof penetrations like plumbing vent pipes. All flashing patches should be sealed with a fully-glued double layer of EPDM.

Self-Adhering EPDM

Self-adhering EPDM membrane has recently become available, eliminating the need to field-apply adhesive.

Seams

Splice seams together with either splicing adhesive or seam tape.

Option 1: Splicing Adhesive

- Allow for a 6-in. overlap.

- Adhere the bottom (downhill) sheet into the deck first.

Figure 63. Troubleshooting Built-Up Roofing

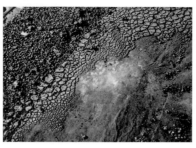

Blistering (left) indicates that the built-up roofing wasn't installed properly. **Alligatoring** (center) is caused by lack of gravel in the flood coat. The surface of the roof has dried out and is starting to deteriorate. **Ponding** (right) is caused by the lack of positive drainage — due to either poor roof design and/or installation or to settlement of the roof structure.

- Carefully clean the overlapping surfaces with white gas or a cleaning solvent recommended by the EPDM manufacturer.

- Then brush the special splicing adhesive onto both mating surfaces. When gluing the top sheet, be careful not to get any adhesive on the overlap area.

- When adhesive is dry to the touch, carefully roll the top piece into place.

- Make sure not to wrinkle or stretch the material, since this puts a built-in stress on the seam.

- Roll the seam with a hand roller to get 100% adhesion.

- Apply a bead of a special lap caulk to the edge of the seam to keep water out.

Option 2: Seam Tape

- Clean and prime the mating surfaces.

- Apply the tape (a 6-in.-wide, two-sided tape with a release paper on one side) to the bottom sheet, and hand-roll it with the release paper in place.

- Then fold the lapping piece over the seam and pull the release paper off the tape as you press the top piece into place.

- Carefully trim the top sheet before sticking it down. Its edge should be parallel to and 1/8 in. back from the edge of the seam tape.

- The edge can then be finished with lap caulk or left as is, since the exposed edge of the seam tape acts as a water stop.

EPDM Edge Details

There are a variety of ways to detail roof edges. Contact your EPDM supplier for installation specs.

Roof-to-brick. Where a roof meets a brick wall, glue the EPDM to the brick 8- to 12-in. up and secure it with an aluminum termination bar (**Figure 60**, page 65).

Roof-to-wood. For a wood-sided wall, run the EPDM behind the bottom course of siding.

Corners. Where the roof meets an inside corner of a sidewall or parapet, you can either fold the corner or slit the membrane and patch (**Figure 61**, page 66). At outside corners, a patch is always necessary.

Penetrations Through EPDM

For waterproofing roof penetrations, use uncured EPDM, which comes in narrow rolls designed for patching and flashing applications. Unlike cured EPDM, uncured EPDM has no memory. When you stretch and glue it around a vent pipe, for instance, it forms itself to the shape of the pipe (**Figure 62**, page 67).

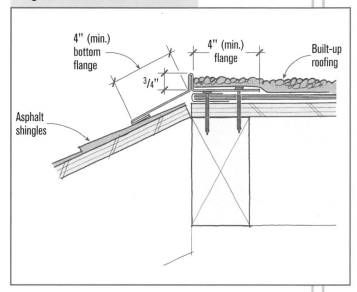

Figure 64. Flat Roof Transition

4" (min.) bottom flange
4" (min.) flange
Built-up roofing
3/4"
Asphalt shingles

Patching EPDM

Patches require two layers of flashing membrane — a smaller first layer and a wider top layer that completely covers the bottom layer. Patches and flashing are glued with splicing adhesive.

Built-up Roofs

The most common encounter residential contractors have with built-up roofs (BUR) is when one is leaking. The most common problems are shown in **Figure 63**.

Figure 65. Patching a Built-up Roof

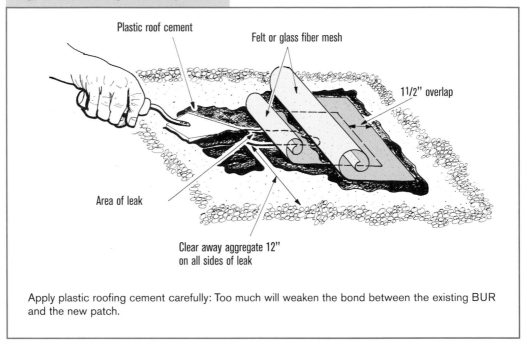

Plastic roof cement

Felt or glass fiber mesh

11/2" overlap

Area of leak

Clear away aggregate 12" on all sides of leak

Apply plastic roofing cement carefully: Too much will weaken the bond between the existing BUR and the new patch.

Leaks aren't always where they seem to be. With a membrane roof, there's a fair chance a leak will be right above the wet spots on the ceiling. With a BUR, however, water can travel through the plies and emerge almost anywhere.

Blistering usually indicates that a built-up roof wasn't installed right. Dirt or moisture may have gotten between the plies during installation, fasteners may not have been driven tightly enough,

or the contractor may have used incompatible materials. Isolated blisters can be fixed following the patching procedure above. If the roof is covered with them, however, you may have to tear it off and start over.

Alligatoring means that the surface of the roof has dehydrated and begun to come apart. If the damage is minor, and if the roofing felts haven't yet hardened, you may be able to restore them with a mineral rubber resurfacer and sealant. If the felts have dried out, apply a primer first. Whatever the scope of the repair, remove all gravel first.

Lack of gravel is what causes alligatoring. One of the functions of a gravel layer is to protect the surface of a built-up roof from the sun's ultraviolet rays, which cause the roof to dry out. If the gravel wears away, the roof won't be far behind.

Ponding water may be caused by a deflection of the roof frame. Ponding can cut the life of a roof by half. Unfortunately, there's not much you can do about it short of a radical restructuring of the roof frame.

Slope transitions. Flat built-up roofs that meet a sloped roof must have a gravel stop to prevent the asphalt flood coat and gravel from migrating down the sloped roof (**Figure 64**, page 69).

Patching a Built-Up Roof

Small BUR repairs can be accomplished using plastic roofing cement and felt (**Figure 65**).

Surface Prep

Clear away the aggregate in the top or "flood" coat with the claw of a hammer or, for larger areas, use a chipping bar (be careful not to damage the existing BUR membrane below the coatings). Smaller stones can be scrubbed away with a wire brush.

Felt Patch

- Use a minimum of two layers of felt or glass fiber mesh to repair BUR. The bottom layer should be $1^1/2$ in. smaller around the edges than the top layer, so that each will bond separately to the existing membrane.

- Apply the patch with a thin coat of plastic roofing cement.

Modified Bitumen Patch

High-quality repairs also can be made with a single layer of modified bitumen.

- Heat the membrane on a scrap of plywood with a propane torch.

- Then apply it over the hole, being careful not to wrinkle it.

Flashing

Flashing materials should be at least as durable as the roof covering. For example, it would not make sense to flash a 100-year-old slate roof with thin aluminum. Once the aluminum begins to leak, the slates would have to be torn off to replace it. Copper flashing would cost more initially, but because it could last as long as the roof, its life cycle costs would be lower.

Figure 66. Eaves Flashing

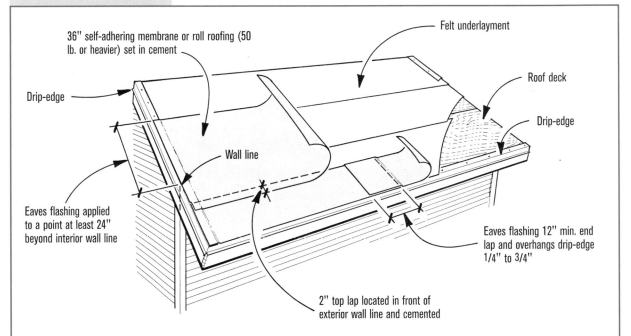

36" self-adhering membrane or roll roofing (50 lb. or heavier) set in cement

Felt underlayment

Roof deck

Drip-edge

Drip-edge

Wall line

Eaves flashing applied to a point at least 24" beyond interior wall line

Eaves flashing 12" min. end lap and overhangs drip-edge 1/4" to 3/4"

2" top lap located in front of exterior wall line and cemented

In cold climates, an eaves flashing is recommended as back-up protection against leaks from ice dams. (To prevent ice dams completely, address the ventilation and insulation issues in the attic. See "Roof Ventilation," pages 90-94.) Self-adhering bituminous membranes are preferred since they seal around nail penetrations.

Figure 67. Roofing Cement Types

Material	Characteristics	Uses	Cautions
Plastic asphalt cement (flashing cement)	Thick consistency; won't flow when hot or become brittle when cold; remains flexible enough when dry to expand and contract with the structure	Gluing down flashing assemblies, caulking joints, and minor repairs	Incompatible with roll roofing
Lap cement	Thinner than plastic cement; brushable	Makes a waterproof bond between layers of roll roofing	Shouldn't be used on asphalt shingles
Quick-setting asphalt adhesive cement	More adhesive than plastic asphalt cement	Used to glue down strip shingles on shallow slopes	–

Figure 68. Minimum Thickness for Flashing Materials

Material	Base or Step and Counterflashing	Wall Openings Head & Sill	Roof Edges, Ridges, and Hips	Crickets, Valleys, or Gutters	Roof Penetrations
Aluminum	.019"	.019"	.019"	.019"	.040"
Galv. Steel	26 gauge	26 gauge	24 gauge	24 gauge	24 gauge
Copper	16 oz.	10 oz.	16 oz.	16 oz.	16 oz.
Lead	1 1/2 lb.	2 1/2 lb.	3 lb.	3 lb.	3 lb.
Painted Terne	20 lb.	40 lb.	20 lb.	40 lb.	40 lb.

Asphalt-Based Eaves flashing

Most roofing systems can be installed over asphalt eaves flashings and roofing cement.

Eaves Flashing

An eaves flashing is a minimum 3-ft.-wide bituminous membrane that's installed beneath the roof covering at the lower edge of a sloped roof

(**Figure 66**, page 72). It's used in regions with design temperatures of 0°F or cooler as a secondary defense against leakage from ice dams.

Not a cure for ice dams. Although some codes require eaves flashings, remember that they're merely a back-up; the only proven cure for ice dams is proper insulation and ventilation (see "Ice Dams," page 93).

Roofing Cement

Although roofing cement has many uses, it's not a substitute for flashing. Also, not all roofing cement is alike. The three main types are *plastic asphalt*

Figure 69. Galvanic Series

Active

1. Zinc
2. Aluminum
3. Steel
4. Iron
5. Nickel
6. Tin
7. Lead
8. Brass
9. Copper
10. Stainless Steel

Passive

The galvanic series ranks metals from active to passive. In a galvanic couple, the more active metal sacrifices itself to protect the more passive one. The farther apart the two metals in the series, the greater the potential for corrosion.

Figure 70. Galvanic Corrosion Between Construction Metals

	Zinc	Alum.	Iron/ Steel	Gal. Steel	Lead	Brass/ Bronze	Copper	Stainless Steel
Zinc	–	0	2	0	0	2	2	2
Aluminum	0	–	1	0	1	2	2	0
Galv. Steel	0	0	1	–	0	1	1	1
Lead	0	1	0	0	–	1	1	1
Copper	2	2	2	1	1	1	–	2

0 = Galvanic action minimal. Metals may come into contact under normal conditions.

1 = Galvanic action possible under some conditions or over long duration.

2 = Strong galvanic action, so direct contact not recommended.

For best results, never combine metal flashings with a 1 or 2 corrosion rating.

Figure 71. Closed Valley Details

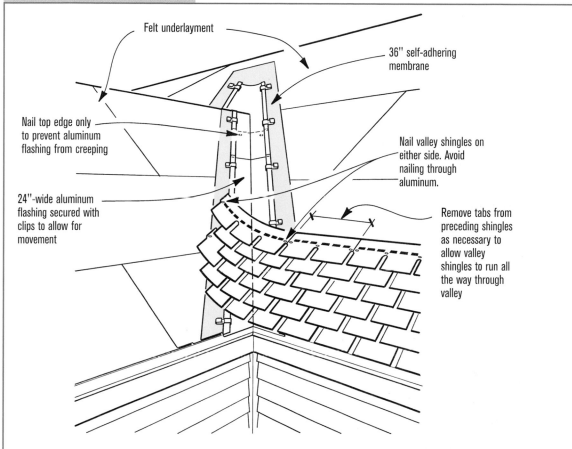

Felt underlayment

36" self-adhering membrane

Nail top edge only to prevent aluminum flashing from creeping

Nail valley shingles on either side. Avoid nailing through aluminum.

24"-wide aluminum flashing secured with clips to allow for movement

Remove tabs from preceding shingles as necessary to allow valley shingles to run all the way through valley

Use a built-up multi-layer flashing system for a more dependable valley. Avoid nailing through the aluminum valley, which would not allow the flashing to expand and contract with temperature changes. The shingles that run through the valley are laid out so that nails can be placed on either side of the aluminum.

cement, *lap cement*, and *asphalt adhesive cement*. Use each according to **Figure 67**, page 73.

Flashing Metals

The most familiar residential flashing metals are aluminum, galvanized steel, zinc, lead, and copper. Which one to use depends on the roofing material and the surrounding environment. Galvanized steel and aluminum are more than adequate for most asphalt roofs, for example, but they won't last as long as a good slate or tile roof. Copper and lead are more durable but also much more expensive.

Gauge Thickness

Whatever the metal, be sure it's thick enough for the job. See **Figure 68**, page 73.

Durability of Metal Flashings

The longevity of any flashing depends on the environment. For example, the alloy used in an aluminum or copper step flashing will corrode quickly when exposed to salt. Therefore, do not use aluminum or copper flashing near the ocean. Use zinc instead — it's not harmed by salt. Lead and copper, on the other hand, stand up well to urban air pollutants, while zinc and galvanized steel do not.

Copper and Cedar Caution

There has been some speculation that the acids in cedar and redwood might corrode copper flashings in a damp environment. This hasn't been proven, but for the time being the cedar

Figure 72. Asphalt Woven Valley

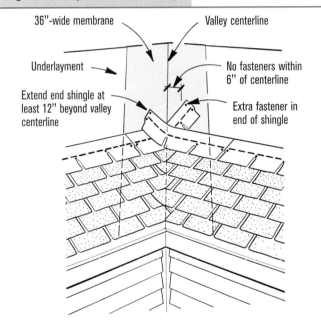

- 36"-wide membrane
- Valley centerline
- Underlayment
- No fasteners within 6" of centerline
- Extend end shingle at least 12" beyond valley centerline
- Extra fastener in end of shingle

Woven valleys can be installed on roof slopes of 4:12 or greater. Caution: In some regions, moss accumulates between the shingle cutouts and impairs water run-off. Keep nails a minimum of 6 in. away from the center of the valley to prevent leakage (8 in. or more away on low-sloped roofs with valleys facing prevailing winds and in regions with annual freeze-thaw cycles).

industry recommends that copper nails be avoided and that copper valleys be made from 16-ounce copper, minimum. To isolate wood shingles from a copper valley, use a cant strip.

Galvanic Corrosion

When dissimilar metals come into contact in the presence of moisture, a small electrical current flows between them, corroding one metal while protecting the other. This is known as a galvanic couple. The speed and direction of the current — and thus the rate of corrosion — is determined by each metal's place on the galvanic series (**Figure 69**, page 74).

Some metals can be used together — lead and galvanized steel, for example — with minimal problems, while other metals — such as copper and aluminum — should never be used together (**Figure 70**, page 74).

The Area Effect

Galvanic corrosion takes place when the anode gives up its electrons to the cathode — the faster the exchange, the faster the corrosion. Exactly how fast depends, in part, on the relative amounts of each metal. The larger the area of the cathode in relation to the

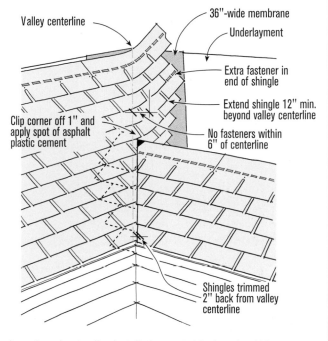

Figure 73. Asphalt Closed-Cut Valley

Valley centerline

36"-wide membrane

Underlayment

Extra fastener in end of shingle

Extend shingle 12" min. beyond valley centerline

Clip corner off 1" and apply spot of asphalt plastic cement

No fasteners within 6" of centerline

Shingles trimmed 2" back from valley centerline

In a closed-cut valley installation, cut shingles should be on the side of the roof that has the greater runoff (the steeper or longer roof plane). You don't want the cut shingles to buck water from any "wash-over" that may occur due to unequal amounts of runoff.

anode, the more intense the coupling, and the faster the corrosion.

The area effect explains why an aluminum nail in a copper flashing corrodes much faster than an aluminum flashing fastened with a copper nail. In the latter case, the nail exerts a very small load on the flashing, while the flashing spreads the load over a relatively large area.

Figure 74. Asphalt Open-Cut Valley

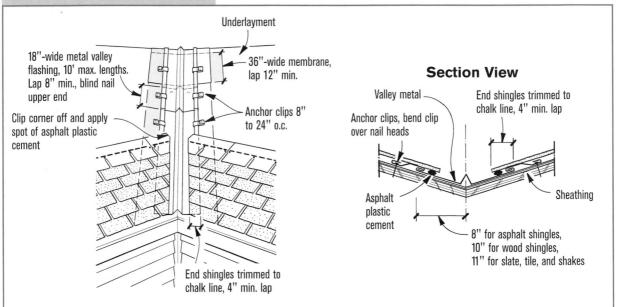

18"-wide metal valley flashing, 10' max. lengths. Lap 8" min., blind nail upper end

Underlayment

36"-wide membrane, lap 12" min.

Anchor clips 8" to 24" o.c.

Clip corner off and apply spot of asphalt plastic cement

Section View

Valley metal

End shingles trimmed to chalk line, 4" min. lap

Anchor clips, bend clip over nail heads

Asphalt plastic cement

Sheathing

8" for asphalt shingles, 10" for wood shingles, 11" for slate, tile, and shakes

End shingles trimmed to chalk line, 4" min. lap

For asphalt shingles, a double layer of roll roofing is adequate for flashing. With other roofing materials, metal flashing is recommended. The metal should be formed with a "W"-shaped splash diverter, especially in valleys where the adjoining roof areas are of unequal size and slope.

Galvanizing

Galvanic corrosion is the secret behind galvanizing. The zinc coating on a piece of galvanized steel is sacrificial, which means it gives way to protect the underlying steel. Because zinc is close to steel on the galvanic series, the reaction takes place slowly enough to give the steel long protection. Once the galvanized coating wears away, the underlying steel begins to rust.

Hot-Dipped vs. Electrogalvanized

Hot-dipping differs from electrogalvanizing in that the former diffuses the zinc part way into the steel's surface, while the latter just leaves a surface coating of zinc. Therefore, hot-dipped galvanized materials last longer than electrogalvanized before the base metal begins to corrode.

Valley Flashing Details

Valleys can be open, closed, or woven (in the case of asphalt shingles), but it's almost always worthwhile to provide more than one level of protection at this juncture. **Figure 71**, page 75, illustrates a "belt and suspenders" approach to valleys that is prudent in harsh climates.

Figure 75. Valley Cleats

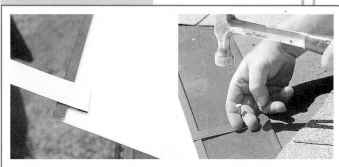

To allow the aluminum flashing to expand and contract, use a site-bent hem-and-clip system to secure valley flashing. Place 2 ft. o.c. at the edge of the flashing.

Figure 76. Flashing Against Walls

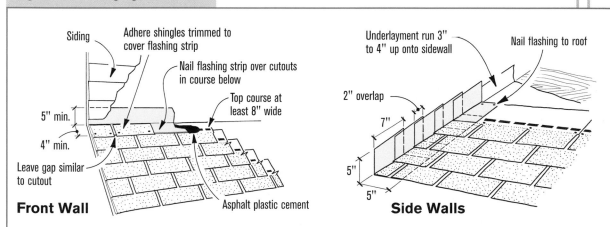

Front Wall

Siding · Adhere shingles trimmed to cover flashing strip · Nail flashing strip over cutouts in course below · Top course at least 8" wide · 5" min. · 4" min. · Leave gap similar to cutout · Asphalt plastic cement

Side Walls

Underlayment run 3" to 4" up onto sidewall · Nail flashing to root · 2" overlap · 7" · 5" · 5"

Front wall: Plan shingle layout so that the last course is at least 8 in. wide. Install continuous metal flashing over the last course and set in asphalt plastic cement. Do not nail the strip to the wall. Apply an additional row of trimmed shingles set in asphalt plastic cement. **Side walls:** Step flashing should be 2 in. longer than the exposure of the roof shingles in order for the step flashings to overlap approximately 2 in. In regions with severe weather, headlaps of 3 in. are common. The headlap should be made from compatible material that has a design life equal to or longer than that of the roofing material. Use 26-gauge (min.) metal for step flashing.

Figure 77. Counterflashing

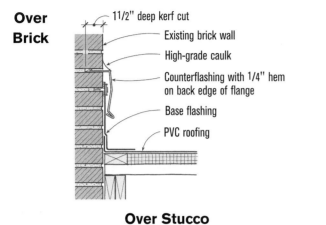

Over Brick

- 1 1/2" deep kerf cut
- Existing brick wall
- High-grade caulk
- Counterflashing with 1/4" hem on back edge of flange
- Base flashing
- PVC roofing

Over Stucco

- Stucco
- High-grade caulk
- Felt underlayment overlaps counter-flashing
- Counterflashing
- Step flashing
- Shingles

Over brick: Counterflashing should be set at a minimum of 1 1/2 inches into the mortar joint. **Over stucco:** Caulk is never enough to seal between stucco and metal sidewall flashing. Use a drip screed as a counterflashing instead.

Woven Valleys

Woven valleys can be quite durable if done right.

- Shingles must extend at least 12 in. beyond the centerline (**Figure 72**, page 76).

- Before shingling, line the valley with 55-lb. roll roofing or with self-adhering eaves membrane.

Closed Valleys

Closed valleys have clean lines, but if done wrong they can trap ice and debris.

The covering course of a closed valley must be cut back a couple of inches from the centerline so that water flows away from the cut edge rather than into it (**Figure 73**, page 77).

Open Valleys

On an asphalt roof, an open valley may be lined with two layers of roll roofing. On all other roofs, metal valley flashing is the only long-term choice (**Figure 74**, page 78).

Some critical aspects of a metal valley flashing are its width, length, the configuration of its centerline and edges, and the way that it's fastened.

Width. A valley must channel runoff from two roofs, while having a shallower slope than either. It's critical that the valley be designed to handle the flow:

- At the peak, a valley should be 5 or 6 in. wide on either side of the centerline.

Figure 78. Gable Dormer Flashing

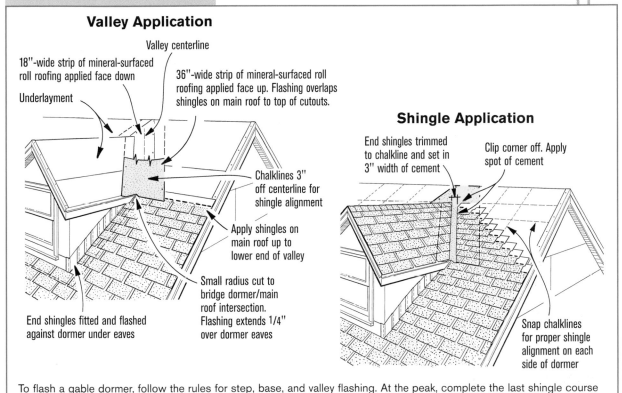

Valley Application

Valley centerline

18"-wide strip of mineral-surfaced roll roofing applied face down

36"-wide strip of mineral-surfaced roll roofing applied face up. Flashing overlaps shingles on main roof to top of cutouts.

Underlayment

Shingle Application

End shingles trimmed to chalkline and set in 3" width of cement

Clip corner off. Apply spot of cement

Chalklines 3" off centerline for shingle alignment

Apply shingles on main roof up to lower end of valley

Small radius cut to bridge dormer/main roof intersection. Flashing extends 1/4" over dormer eaves

End shingles fitted and flashed against dormer under eaves

Snap chalklines for proper shingle alignment on each side of dormer

To flash a gable dormer, follow the rules for step, base, and valley flashing. At the peak, complete the last shingle course on the main roof before applying the dormer ridge shingles.

- As it descends toward the eaves, it should widen 1/8 in. for every foot of run.

Length. To avoid excessive expansion and contraction, use 8- to 10-ft. lengths of metal, maximum, for valley flashing.

- Avoid using aluminum, which expands at a greater rate than other metals.

- Lap sections 8 in. minimum.

Centerline. When a steep roof intersects a shallow one, water cascading down the steep roof can overshoot the valley and run up beneath the shingles on the shallow one. Roofs like this need a valley flashing with a crimped centerline. The steeper the roof, the more critical the crimp will be.

Figure 79. Shed Dormer Flashing

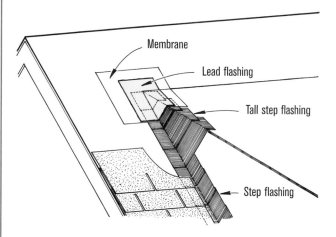

The top corners of a shed dormer are particularly susceptible to leaks. Use tall pieces of sidewall flashing, combined with a lead flashing patch.

Figure 80. Cricket Construction

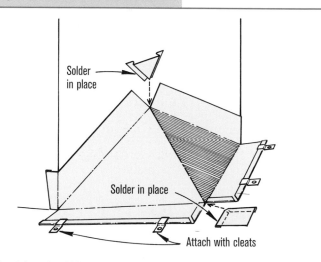

A cricket should be built of plywood, then covered by a single piece of metal. To permit expansion and contraction of the large piece of metal, attach it to the roof deck with cleats.

Edge treatments. Like all roof flashings, valley flashings should have hemmed edges. Not only do these shed water more effectively, but by holding the shingles away from the flashing, they prevent capillary suction from drawing water up under the shingles.

Ridge treatment. Valleys that meet at a ridge should be soldered to one another. However, this connection may break when the valley metal expands and contracts. Best practice calls for covering the connection at the ridge with a moldable piece of lead flashing.

Fasteners. Metal valleys can be fastened with nails or cleats at 2 ft. o.c. (**Figure 75**, page 79).

- Cleats are better; they won't become fatigued and shear when the metal expands and contracts.

- When using nails, place them at least 5 in. away from the valley's center to prevent leaks.

The Code on Valleys

CABO requires that metal valleys be fabricated from no less than No. 28-gauge corrosion-resistant sheet metal.

- For asphalt shingles, valley flashing must extend at least 8 in. on either side of the centerline.

- For wood shingles, the wings of a valley must extend 10 in. each way.

- For slate, tile, and wood shakes, a valley must extend 11 in. each way.

- Sections of flashing must have an end lap of at least 4 in. for wood shingles and shakes, and at least 6 in. for slate and tile roofs.

Roof-to-wall Flashing

Front Wall Flashing Checklist

- Install shingles up the roof until you reach the base of the vertical wall. Adjust the exposure of the last few courses, if necessary, so the last course is at least 8 in. wide (**Figure 76**, page 79).

- Cut and bend a continuous metal flashing strip that extends at least 5 in. up the vertical wall and at least 4 in. over the last shingle course.

- When installing the metal flashing strip over the last course of shingles, embed it in roofing cement and nail it to the roof only.

- Do not nail the flashing strip to the wall.

- Apply an additional row of shingles — trimmed to the width of the flashing — over the flashing and

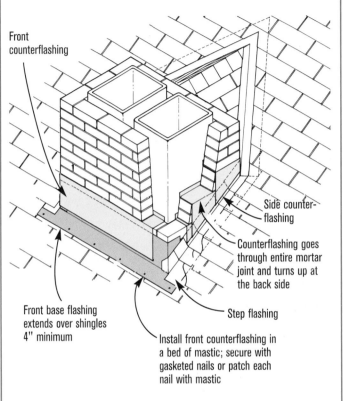

Figure 81. Chimney Flashing

Front counterflashing

Side counterflashing

Counterflashing goes through entire mortar joint and turns up at the back side

Step flashing

Front base flashing extends over shingles 4" minimum

Install front counterflashing in a bed of mastic; secure with gasketed nails or patch each nail with mastic

Never attach a flashing to both the chimney and the roof. The base flashing is attached to the roof only, the counterflashing to the chimney only. This allows the house to move independently of the chimney.

embedded in asphalt plastic roofing cement.

Sidewall Flashing Checklist

Shingle roofs (asphalt, slate, or wood) that butt against vertical walls are best protected by metal step flashing placed over the end of each shingle course (**Figure** 76, page 79).

- Cut step flashing pieces to be 10 in. long and 2 in. wider than the shingle exposure (e.g., 7 in. for roof shingles with a 5-in. exposure).

Figure 82. Skylight Opening

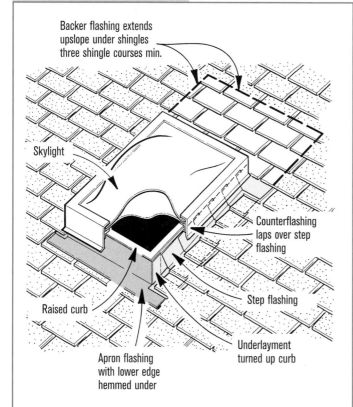

Backer flashing extends upslope under shingles three shingle courses min.

Skylight

Counterflashing laps over step flashing

Step flashing

Raised curb

Underlayment turned up curb

Apron flashing with lower edge hemmed under

Unless it comes with a premanufactured flashing assembly, a skylight should rest on a curb or box that protrudes at least 6 in. above the roof surface.

- Bend the 10-in. length to extend 5 in. over the roof deck and 5 in. up the wall surface.

- Place each step flashing piece about $1/4$ in. above the bottom edge of the shingle that will overlap it — just enough so that the flashing piece is not visible when the overlapping shingle is in place.

- Because the metal strips are 2 in. wider than the exposure of the shingles (e.g., 7 in. for roof shingles laid with a 5-in. exposure), each step flashing piece will overlap the one on the course below by 2 in.

- Nail flashing to the roof deck only. Do not nail flashing to the wall.

- Bring wood siding down over the vertical sections of the step flashing to serve as counterflashing. Do not nail siding into step flashing.

Counterflashing

Stucco and brick siding must have a counterflashing over a step flashing or continuous wall flashing strip (**Figure** 77, page 80).

Counterflashing Brick

The most common failure of flashing over brick is caused by not setting the flange deep enough. Bring the flashing all the way through the brick in new construction. Over existing brick, set the counterflashing a minimum $1^1/2$ inches into the mortar joint, as shown in **Figure 77**, page 80.

Counterflashing Stucco

In the case of stucco siding, the drip screed functions as the counter-flashing.

Flashing Gable Dormers

A gable, or doghouse, dormer includes base, step, counter, and valley flash-ings, as shown in **Figure 78**, page 81.

- When using metal open valleys on a gable dormer, make sure they're soldered together at the peak, then cover with a lead patch.

- Shingle the main roof before shin-gling over the dormer ridge.

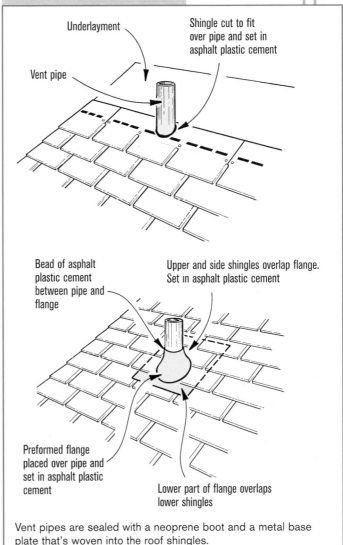

Figure 83. Vent Pipe Flashing

Underlayment

Shingle cut to fit over pipe and set in asphalt plastic cement

Vent pipe

Bead of asphalt plastic cement between pipe and flange

Upper and side shingles overlap flange. Set in asphalt plastic cement

Preformed flange placed over pipe and set in asphalt plastic cement

Lower part of flange overlaps lower shingles

Vent pipes are sealed with a neoprene boot and a metal base plate that's woven into the roof shingles.

Flashing Shed Dormers

Shed dormers require a continuous strip of flashing along the top of the lower roof plane where it meets the steeper roof plane. Also, they require sidewall flashings. A critical juncture that often fails is where these two flashings meet. Use taller pieces of step flashing toward the top, so the pieces can be bent over the dormer roof to help keep out snow and wind-blown rain (**Figure 79**, page 82).

Flashing Chimneys

Chimneys should be surrounded by base, step, and counter-flashings, as shown in **Figure 81**, page 83.

Chimney Cricket

Where a chimney breaks through the field of a roof, best practice calls for using a cricket to divert water away from the upper edge on the chimney. Crickets can be covered with the same material as the rest of the roof, using metal valley flashing where it meets the main roof. Or better still, fashion a metal cricket cover with 20-gauge metal as shown in **Figure 80**, page 82.

Flashing Skylights

Most skylight flashings come as a kit from the manufacturer. Skylights without flashing kits should be mounted on a curb and flashed as shown in **Figure 82**, page 84.

Flashing Vent Pipe Penetrations

Vent pipes on wood and asphalt roofs are usually flashed using a preassembled metal pan with a rubber boot. Order the unit according to the outside diameter of the vent pipe and install it as shown in **Figure 83**, page 85. For slate and tile roofs, a malleable lead jacket will last longer.

Gutters

Some cold-climate builders avoid gutters because of their reputation for getting caked with ice. The ice bends them, pops their seams, and sometimes pulls them off the house. Yet without gutters, any water not handled at the roof line must be managed on the ground.

Where to Use Gutters

- Gutters do the most good in heavy rainfall areas and on buildings with little or no overhang.

- Gutters should always be used where houses are built on clay and other frost-susceptible soils (some expansive clays can crack a foundation without freezing; they need only be wet).

- Use gutters wherever roof run-off creates a splashback problem that might accelerate the deterioration of entry steps, decks, and siding.

Figure 84. Gutter Location

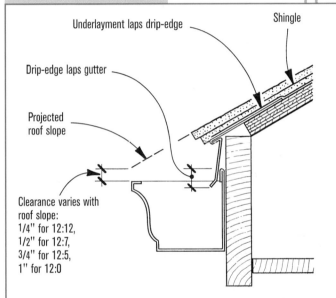

Underlayment laps drip-edge

Shingle

Drip-edge laps gutter

Projected roof slope

Clearance varies with roof slope:
1/4" for 12:12,
1/2" for 12:7,
3/4" for 12:5,
1" for 12:0

Place gutters below the roof's slope-line so that ice and snow can slide by.

- Gutters go a long way toward solving basement water problems. For this reason they are required by code in some places.

Figure 85. Hanger Types

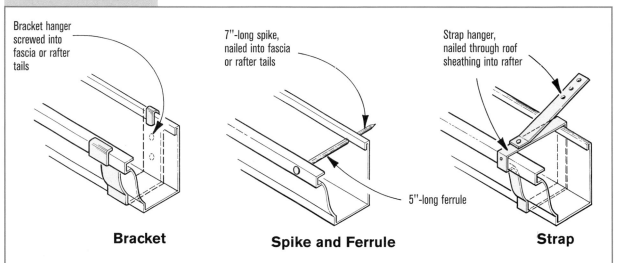

Bracket hanger screwed into fascia or rafter tails

7"-long spike, nailed into fascia or rafter tails

Strap hanger, nailed through roof sheathing into rafter

5"-long ferrule

Bracket   **Spike and Ferrule**   **Strap**

The "ogee" gutter profile is the most commonly used in residential construction. The hangers shown here are readily available for the "ogee" gutter. Expansion joints are needed for every 40 ft. (max.) of run.

Without Gutters

If you don't use gutters, it's best to cap the backfill with an impermeable soil layer around the house and slope the grade away from the house at least one inch per foot. Rectangular flagstones laid below the roof's drip line are another option: they'll prevent erosion and cause most of the water to splash away from the foundation.

Gutter installation

Old-style wood and yankee gutters caused a lot of damage because when they leaked, the water backed up into the eaves. This promotes decay in the rafter ends and the soffit. Modern metal and vinyl gutters do a much better job, but there is still the potential for problems if the gutters are not installed with the proper clearances (**Figure 84**, page 87).

In cold climates, the outside edges of all gutters should fall below the roof's slope line so snow and ice can slide clear. The shallower the roof, the more clearance is needed.

Hanger Types

There are three common hanger types (**Figure 85**). Of these, strap-type hangers that hold the gutter away from the fascia provide the most protection against decay.

Installation Details

- Aluminum gutter runs should have an expansion joint every 40 ft. of straight run since the gutter will expand and contract $1/8$ in. or more over that span.

- Gutters should slope at least $1/16$ in. per foot of run. It is important to move the water quickly away from the foundation with either a subsurface pipe or splash blocks and by sloping the grade at the surface.

- The number of downspouts a roof needs will depend on the size of the conductor pipe. Allow 1 sq. in. of downspout cross-section for every 100 sq. ft. of roof area. Place the downspouts at least 20 ft. apart but no more than 50 ft. apart.

Roof Ventilation

Roof ventilation is required on sloped roofs by all building codes and some roofing material warranties.

Why Ventilate?

Ventilation does several things:

- Ventilation reduces attic temperatures in the summer by as much as

30°F. This extends shingle life and cuts cooling bills.

- Ventilation helps rid the attic of any excess moisture.

- By keeping the roof uniformly cold in winter, ventilation helps prevent ice damming.

Attic ventilation works best where there's an airtight ceiling plane — that is, one that prevents warm, moist interior air from rising up from the house below.

Sizing Vents

Most codes specify a net-free vent area (NFVA) of $1/150$ of the attic area if the ceiling has no vapor retarder, or $1/300$ with a vapor retarder. The ventilation area should be split $50/50$ between low and high vents, preferably soffit and ridge vents.

NFVA is the combined area of all unobstructed ventilation openings. To calculate the actual vent area required, start with the required NFVA, then

Figure 86. Typical Net-Free Vent Areas (NFVA)

Vent Covering	Vent Area Multiplier
$1/4$-inch mesh hardware cloth	1.00
$1/8$-inch mesh screen	1.25
#16 mesh screen, with or without plain metal louvers	2.00
Wood louvers and $1/4$-inch mesh hardware cloth	2.00
Wood louvers and $1/8$-inch mesh screen	2.25
Wood louvers and #16 screen	3.00

This multiplier tells how many square feet of vent area is needed to give 1 sq. ft. of net-free vent area.

enlarge it to compensate for screens and louvers. For example, vents with $1/8$-in. mesh insect screen should be enlarged by 25% (**Figure 86**).

Calculate vent area:

$$NFVA = \text{Area of Vent Opening X}$$
$$\text{Vent area Multiplier}$$

Compare to attic area:

$$\text{Actual Vent Area} =$$
$$\frac{\text{Sq. Ft. of Attic Floor}}{NFVA}$$

Actual vent area must equal .0066 or more (without ceiling vapor barrier) or .0033 (with ceiling vapor barrier).

Vent Types and Location

For good attic ventilation, the vents should be evenly divided between intake and exhaust (**Figure 87**).

Soffit and Ridge Vents

For best performance, locate vents at the soffit (intake) and ridge (exhaust).

Do not use a ridge vent without soffit vents. A ridge vent without soffit vents could make matters worse in windy conditions by pulling moist air from

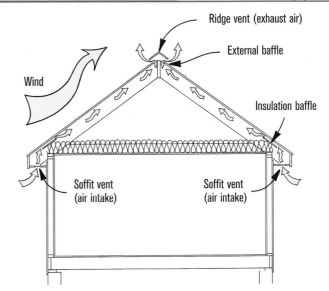

Figure 87. Roof Vent Location

Ridge vent (exhaust air)

External baffle

Wind

Insulation baffle

Soffit vent (air intake)

Soffit vent (air intake)

Roof ventilation should be divided about 50/50 between low and high locations. For best performance, use a soffit vent and baffled ridge vent to allow for both intake and exhaust.

inside the house, and adding moisture to the attic. Research suggests that somewhat oversized soffit vents are a good idea because they provide insurance against this type of leakage.

Gable-End Vents

Gable-end vents do not pull air evenly from all parts of the attic. Use gable-end vents only when soffit vents cannot be installed.

Figure 88. Venting Cathedral Ceilings

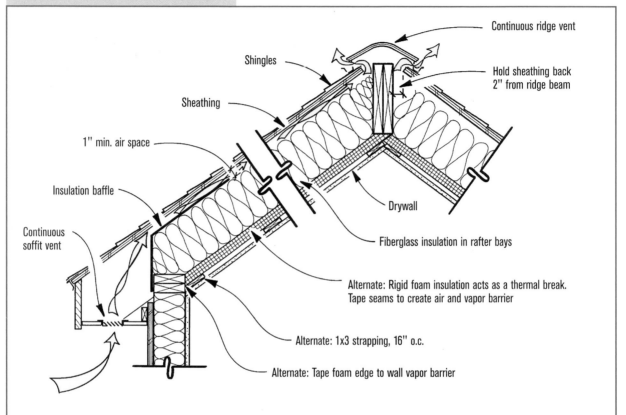

Continuous ridge vent

Shingles

Hold sheathing back 2" from ridge beam

Sheathing

1" min. air space

Insulation baffle

Continuous soffit vent

Drywall

Fiberglass insulation in rafter bays

Alternate: Rigid foam insulation acts as a thermal break. Tape seams to create air and vapor barrier

Alternate: 1x3 strapping, 16" o.c.

Alternate: Tape foam edge to wall vapor barrier

In cathedral ceilings, leave a minimum 2-in. space for airflow between the insulation and the underside of the sheathing.

Use a Baffle

Choose ridge vents with some type of a baffle to deflect windblown rain and snow from infiltrating the vent. Some vents use other mechanisms to restrict the entry of snow and water, although some of these restrict airflow as well.

Cathedral Ceiling Venting

Use the same combination of ridge and soffit vents in a cathedral-type ceiling, leaving a minimum ventilation channel of 2 in. between the top of the insulation and the underside of the sheathing, as in **Figure 88**.

Roof Vent Interruptions

Where roof penetrations such as skylights or chimneys interrupt the airflow from soffit to ridge, cut notches or drill holes in the rafters to let air flow around the obstruction (**Figure 89**).

Ice Dams

When warm air escapes from a structure's conditioned space and finds its way to the back of the roof sheathing, it can melt snow that has collected on the roof. When the melted snow reaches the eaves or other unheated area, it can refreeze and cause an ice dam (**Figure 90**). Melted snow from farther up the roof will then pond behind this dam, back up beneath the shingles, and find its way into the structure.

Ice Dam Prevention

The way to prevent ice dams is to keep the roof sheathing uniformly cold and close to the outside temperature. The best way to do this is to:

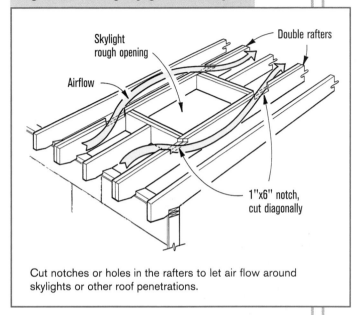

Figure 89. Venting Skylight Rafter Bays

Skylight rough opening

Double rafters

Airflow

1"x6" notch, cut diagonally

Cut notches or holes in the rafters to let air flow around skylights or other roof penetrations.

- Install good attic insulation and ventilation, along with a tight ceiling plane.

- Detail the eaves so they have a full thickness of insulation with ventilation space above. Do not allow insulation to plug the ventilation channel near the eaves.

- Keep heating ducts out of the attic space, since most heating ducts leak at the joints, and will increase attic temperatures.

Figure 90. Ice Dams

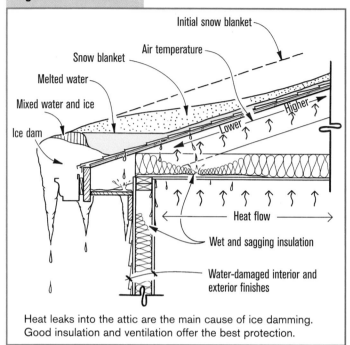

Heat leaks into the attic are the main cause of ice damming. Good insulation and ventilation offer the best protection.

Figure 91. Cold Roof

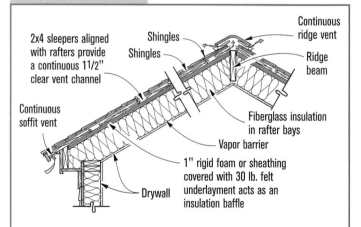

Cathedral or vaulted ceilings in severely cold, snowy climates may require a double-layer "cold" roof to prevent ice dams. The upper vented layer removes warm air that escapes through the insulated lower layer. The outside roof surface remains at the same temperature as the outside ambient air, preventing the freeze-thaw cycle that normally occurs on standard roofs.

The Cold Roof

For cathedral ceilings in very cold and snowy regions, some builders have found it necessary to take roof ventilation a step further, building what's called a cold roof. It consists of two distinct roof layers separated by a 2- to 3-in. air space. A cold roof is capped by a "Boston Ridge" — a large, site-built raised ridge vent with an overhang large enough to keep out snow (**Figure 91**).